Vir-Chew! Dog Bless You!
What Modern Dog Training Taught Me about Living a Good Life

By

Dan Josselyn-Creighton

Table of Contents

Foreword

This is my Love story. That may not be obvious since I started it off with a silly pun on virtue and dogs in the title, but I Love silly puns, I Love dogs and, thanks to my experiences with three special dogs—Kayla, Buffy, and Spike—I Love my life. This book is about how the Love I shared with these three dogs taught me how to cope with the pain of death and Love life again. My hope for this book is that it will help some people learn to Love their lives a little more too. When I look at the world around me, I often get the feeling most people don't Love their lives. Maybe you don't Love yours. I didn't always Love mine. I Loved my life when I was a little kid: playing football with my brothers and my dad; watching cartoons and pro wrestling; talking about life with my mom; reading comic books, fantasy, and science fiction; and playing Dungeons and Dragons with friends. Our family was poor, but we had enough to get by, and my parents were the most Loving people I ever met. I know life was a struggle for them, but they did their best for us, and I had a happy childhood.

I struggled with a few things when I got into high school. I was a late bloomer and sometimes got teased. I also really struggled to figure out if I was gay, straight, or bi. I honestly didn't know. I was very conflicted, confused, and scared. There were no gay or bi kids in my high school who were out of the closet back then. Not one. I didn't date much as a result and spent a lot of time feeling lonely while I was in high school and college.

My loneliness was cured by a Loveable cocker spaniel with a wiggly bum; her name was Kayla. Kayla lived to be nineteen years old, and she was always my baby. I never had children of my own, and I lived alone for ten years, but Kayla didn't let me feel lonely. She was a fun, playful, affectionate dog who made me feel more lucky than lonely. We used to play hide and seek in our condo and take long walks in the park across the street. We both especially Loved it when there was snow on the ground. We would run over early in the morning while the park was covered in a pristine, unbroken sea of white and trample through as much of it as we could until we were tired out and had to walk back home. Neither one of us ever got too old to Love playing in the snow! She was nineteen years old when the picture under the table of contents was taken. That was New Year's Eve 2007, at my sister's house in Massachusetts. On New Year's Day 2008, she died of a stroke in my arms. That was probably the most painful moment of my life up to that point.

Shortly thereafter, my sister and my mom were both diagnosed with cancer. My sister recovered, but my mother's cancer was terminal. I was living in Toronto by then, but I was coming back to Massachusetts as often as I could to visit my family. I was looking for work, and not having much luck, so I decided to take a dog-grooming course. I was still struggling to cope with Kayla's death and decided I wanted to work with dogs the rest of my life. My spouse and I adopted a Shih Tzu Pomeranian puppy named Buffy, after the Vampire Slayer, around the same time. My husband had never had a dog before, so I didn't think it was fair to leave the puppy with him while I drove to Massachusetts practically every weekend, but I also didn't know how well the puppy would handle the drive or meeting so many new people. The first time I took Buffy to meet my parents, I was stressed, sad, and terrified that I was making a mistake bringing her. It was a stressful time for the whole family. My mom knew she was dying and had to be on oxygen all the time. A day or two before I arrived, she also had a fall and bruised her back very badly, so she was stuck in bed, in pain, and waiting to die. I was shaking with fear and sadness when I got to my parents' place. As soon as I opened the door to my parents' apartment, Buffy ran into my mom's room, jumped up on her bed, crawled across her chest, and started licking her face with the frantic, hysterical joy that only a four-month-old puppy can generate. At first, I thought it might be uncomfortable, and I was about to take Buffy off when my mom *yelled*, "No, don't make her stop!" as she burst out laughing. I started laughing, my mom kept laughing, and Buffy was spinning in circles with joy on my mom's chest. It was one of the best memories of my life. Buffy took a moment that was terrifying and painful, and she made it beautiful. I was, and still am, so proud of her.

My grooming experience did not go as well as planned, and I didn't know what to do with my life. Most dogs didn't seem to particularly like being groomed. I was hoping grooming Buffy would be a bonding experience, but instead it was a struggle. I wanted to work with dogs to help me deal with Kayla's death, and instead it became another source of stress to deal with while I was watching my mother slowly die. My mom eventually passed away a little over a year after Kayla did. After my mother died, I continued to struggle as a groomer. I never felt like I was very good at it, and never really felt like I fit in at any of the shops I worked in. I was far away from most of my friends and family, so I didn't have as much support as I was used to either. I eventually had to be treated for depression. The doctor determined it was situational and I was only treated for a year but, for that year at least, I needed help. I was not OK.

I am OK now. I started to learn about modern dog training and behavior, and I fell in Love with it. It helped me teach Buffy, and other dogs, to Love being groomed. It strengthened my relationship with Buffy and helped me deal with the pain of losing Kayla. I started working with dogs because of Kayla. I started to learn about dog training because of my experiences with grooming, and Buffy. I work as a trainer full time now, and we've added a new member of the family, a former street dog and shelter dog named Spike. The business is still small, but it's growing steadily all the time and it's the most rewarding job I've ever had. I may not have gotten off to a great start, but thanks to positive, scientific dog training, I am doing exactly what I want to do with my life. I Love this, and I will Love it forever, just like I will always Love Kayla, Buffy, and Spike.

Introduction

This book is about what modern, scientific dog training has taught me about leading a fulfilling, satisfying, and virtuous life. I think I need to point out right away that I am not as decent and virtuous a person as I wish I was. Like all of us, I've had my share of hard times, haven't always handled them well, and have done many things that I'm ashamed of. I often find myself thinking I'm not a good enough person to write a book like this. We're a flawed species, and I certainly have my share of personal flaws. But I do think my experience as a dog trainer has changed me, and although I am far from perfect, I think I am a better person than I was five years ago. I am definitely happier and more productive. Since I started working as a dog trainer, I have felt like I was on the right track. I know what I want to do with the rest of my life, I know how to do it, and I am confident that I will succeed. This is new for me. I've never had this clarity of purpose and feeling of mission before.

I always wanted to write a book, and have started, but never finished, several. One of the things that always held me back was fear of success, and the lack of privacy people must accept when they put something out for public consumption. I was worried that if my book became more successful than I expected it to be, if I achieved some degree of fame, I wouldn't be able to cope with the pressure. I feared the thought of people picking my work apart publicly, attacking me personally, and making me look foolish. I expected myself and my work to be attacked. I did not believe I was a good enough writer to write this book and expect people to take it seriously. We all feel inadequate sometimes, we've all made mistakes, and we've all done things we're not proud of.

But for all my flaws and insecurities, I know I'm on the right track now. My worst habits (patterns of thought and behavior) are fading or are gone, and I've cultivated new, healthier habits in their place, and I'm not done. I am trying to be a better person every day, and I am still making progress. For the first time in my life, I am confident I will continue to do so. I have overcome my worst fears and insecurities and feel obligated to share what I've learned.

I think it all begins with the Golden Rule. I named my dog-training business Golden Rule Dog Training and use a version of it for our motto: "*Treating every client, canine and human, the way we would like to be treated: with dignity and respect.*" It's not just a slogan or business strategy though, and I don't think it should be limited to clients, or even to just humans. I think it is our duty to treat every sentient being with the same dignity and respect that we want others to show us.

Like many of us, I first learned about the Golden Rule from the church my parents took me to. That's probably obvious if you've perused the table of contents. There are several religious references. You may have noticed seven of the chapters are modeled after the seven Christian virtues, consisting of the three theological virtues of faith, hope, and Love, followed by the four cardinal virtues of prudence, justice, fortitude, and temperance. You may have also noticed that when listing the seven virtues, I chose *not* to use the word faith, but replaced it with the word trust instead. The chapter on trust is the first chapter on the virtues and it includes the line, "You can trust science." The next chapter after the seven virtues revolves around a famous biblical quote from the Sermon on the Mount: "How can you say to your brother, 'Let me take the speck out of your eye,' while there is still a beam in your own eye?" There is also a chapter called "Foundations" that deals extensively with math and science. One of the most frequently noted aspects of modern dog training is that it relies on science, which is exactly why it has been so successful.

So you may be wondering, is this book about dog training, science, Christianity, philosophy, or religion? It's about all those things, and how those things intersect in surprising and hopeful ways. This book is about living a good, virtuous, fulfilling life, and making the world a better, happier place for everyone. We can learn how to do that by looking at science, our history, our culture, and most importantly, at our own lives.

No matter what your view on religion, historically it's one of the ways in which people most frequently discuss virtue and morality. Centuries of philosophical discussions and debates about virtue and morality between some of history's most brilliant minds have taken place in religious contexts. We can't ignore all that. It's also true that no matter what your views on science, you can't function in the modern world without it. It's practically omnipresent in our lives. I'm typing this right now on a computer. Science is the tool we use to build and organize knowledge in the form of testable explanations and predictions about the universe. Science isn't usually thought of as virtuous or moral, but I think an understanding of science can help to make us more virtuous, moral people because it can help to keep us honest. And it's the most trustworthy method for expanding and improving our understanding of the world around us. It can be used for evil or good purposes, but it does represent something true. Rejecting science is foolish and dishonest.

The famous scientist and author Stephen Jay Gould, in his essay "Nonoverlapping Magisteria," tried to argue that we should have separate spheres of influence for religion and science (which he called NOMA for Non-Overlapping MagisteriA), arguing that science is what we should use to uncover truths about the physical world, and religion is what we should use to understand morality and ethics.[1] I Love Stephen Jay Gould, but I can't agree with that. I don't think it's possible to have such a clear dividing line between the two, and it also seems a little dismissive of the contributions atheists and agnostics have made towards our understanding of a virtuous life. But I think his heart was in the right place, because he was following the Golden Rule. He was a non-believer himself, but he *treated those who disagreed with him with the same dignity and respect that he wanted to be treated with.* I hope I can follow his good example with this book.

Throughout history, most of us first learned about the Golden Rule and virtue through our religious upbringing. That's not the only way, but it *is* the way most of us first encountered it. While it is true that all the world's most well-known religions teach a version of the Golden Rule, it's also true that secular, non-religious arguments in favor of it have been made by Kant, Confucius, John Rawls, and many, many more. The Golden Rule pops up everywhere: in every religion, in every culture, in philosophy, and even science, as modern, scientific, dog training clearly shows. One of my heroes, Dr. Sophia Yin, once said: "Now, which way would you rather learn? How many of you would prefer to be nagged? Hey, nobody raised their hand. How many of you would rather be rewarded? Yeah, me too."[2] Those were real eye-opening questions to me. Too often people ask, "How do I get my dog to *blank*?" without even thinking about what the dog wants or needs. It's better to ask, "Why is my dog doing this and what's the fairest way to convince them to do something more appropriate or safer?" To do that, we need to see things from the dog's perspective, and that will hopefully lead us to treating the dog as having its own inherent worth apart from us, and not just as a thing that we own or get something from. In the words of Immanuel Kant's categorical imperative, we should see *all* rational entities as "ends in themselves" and not a means to an end. Other people and other animals are not here merely for our benefit; they are not just things to be used. They are

11

inherently valuable in themselves, just like us, and just like every "rational entity." I don't know to what extent animals, including humans, are rational, but it seems clear according to the best research we have that most, if not all, animals are sentient. It seems likely to me that most sentient animals have at least some capacity for rationality, with humans having the most, and all of them would object to being used if they had a voice.

Rationality was the relevant question for Kant's categorical imperative. For Jeremy Bentham, the father of utilitarianism, the relevant question is "Can they suffer?" making sentience the relevant standard rather than rationality. I am inclined to agree with Bentham here. It's unclear precisely how rational any of us really are, but we all understand what suffering is like, and we don't like it. The ability to reason is a power that we should use responsibly for the well-being of all sentient creatures. It is not an excuse to use less gifted creatures as we see fit, or to disregard their suffering. This does have some far-reaching implications. My belief is our civilization is moving closer to a vegan lifestyle, but it's going to be an awfully slow process, and there's no benefit to berating people into giving up meat for the same reason we don't berate our dogs for their behavior: It probably does more harm than good. Most vegans and vegetarians give up and go back to eating meat because it's extremely hard not to. We're addicted to it. That doesn't make it OK, but it does mean that if we want to change, and we hope others will want to change as well, we can't badger them into it with harsh aversives. That will fail. Instead, we should promote vegan alternatives, patronize their businesses, and prove that some of these options are not only less problematic ethically, but they also have a surprisingly satisfying taste. I'm struggling with this myself right now. I tried giving up meat many, many years ago and I failed. That's why I can't bring myself to insist on a vegan or vegetarian diet yet. We don't judge dogs, cats, or other animals for eating meat because it is a natural compulsion for them. Carnivores like cats cannot survive without eating other animals. We can live without meat, and so can dogs, but it does not come naturally to us; it's hard and, if you aren't careful, dangerous. I am working towards giving up meat again, but I haven't yet. I will though, because it's finally getting easier. There are more vegan and vegetarian options that are healthy and delicious than ever before. Beyond Meat burgers are becoming increasingly popular, and a qualified nutritionist can give you life-changing vegan smoothie recipes that are extremely healthy and delicious. I do believe eventually, possibly even in our lifetime, eating meat will be considered incompatible with decent, virtuous behavior.

To be a decent dog trainer or parent I think you need to be a decent, virtuous person. You do *not* have to be religious to be a decent, virtuous person, and you don't need to be an atheist or agnostic either. I don't want to say specifically what I believe when it comes to religion right now. Too many people will immediately decide you are a fool or a monster if you don't see reality the same way they do. I think we have far too many intensely angry arguments about things that are almost impossible to resolve definitively, politics and religion being the two most obvious. But I think an agreement about what is right, virtuous, and good, while difficult, can be achieved. This book is about the way modern, scientific dog training re-taught me that the lessons I learned about being a good person from my parents (Jean and Joe Josselyn) were always true, and always will be. It's also my hope that writing this book will deepen my own commitment to the virtues I am trying to cultivate and promote in myself. I am using this book to declare publicly: "This is who I am now, and who I will always be." I've found myself. I know who I am and what I want to do with the rest of my life, and I

Love it. There's a comfort and joy in that, which I hope I can share with everyone.

Update: May 2021. Most of this book was written before the pandemic hit. It's been a hard time for most of us. I converted most of my training to online classes, which have worked great, but I miss playing and working directly with other people's dogs. I miss playing darts in pubs with my friends and teammates. I miss hugs. Every year I look forward to visiting my friends and family in Massachusetts for Christmas. Watching kids open Christmas presents is something I look forward to all year, every year. I didn't get to visit my family at all last year. During the summer, we had a series of increasingly awful plumbing emergencies, and had plumbers and maintenance people in and out of our home constantly for several weeks. Having a dozen strangers going in and out of your house can be stressful during the best of times; during a pandemic, it was terrifying. This was also stressful for our dogs, which made it more stressful for us, which made it more stressful for our dogs, and us, in a self-perpetuating stress loop. At one point we went over a week without a functional toilet. There were multiple days I ended up having to defecate into plastic bags. I started to suffer from severe insomnia, sleeping less than three hours per night on average, some nights not at all. I was also very worried about the political situation, especially in the US where one of my siblings was being harassed by a conspiracy theorist neighbor over a bumper sticker she had. Armed insurrectionists took over the Capitol building, a place I worked in as an intern while studying political science in college. I saw the work of democracy being done up close and in person in that building and it was a profoundly moving experience. Then we all had to watch helplessly, live on TV, as it all started to come undone. I had serious doubts as to whether democracy in America was going to survive. I still have serious doubts about that. It was all traumatic. I have no doubt I was suffering from depression. I didn't get a formal diagnosis, but I did struggle with situational depression once before, and I know what it feels like. I knew I was feeling it again.

The biggest bright spot during this time was also a source of stress: our new rescue dog Spike. Spike was a street dog that ended up in a shelter for over six months with no adoption applications. He was terrified of being groomed or vetted, so his hair was a mess. He also made a lot of strange sounds that at first I thought were growls. Sometimes they were, but other times his body language and behavior seemed to indicate he was happy. We've had him for over a year and a half now, and we now know these sounds are like a cat purring, or moaning with pleasure, like when you finally scratch a bothersome itch, or stretch out tensed up muscles. It took a lot of work to teach him not to be afraid of things like nail trims and being examined on the table. He also had a difficult time getting used to my partner Jeff, whom he bit the day he met him. Fortunately, that didn't take very long, and within a few days Spike was sitting on Jeff's lap. Buffy and Spike had a couple polite disagreements early on over resource guarding, but generally they seemed to get along pretty well together. They didn't play with each other very often, and never for very long, but I think they both appreciate having a familiar butt to sniff.

Spike did have a hard time with all the plumbers and maintenance people we had going in and out all day, every day. Buffy did too, but it was harder for Spike. He lost some of the progress he had made, and I was feeling bad about that. I felt like I was doing a bad job. Spike still clearly Loved us though. Whenever the stress of caring for a particularly challenging dog during a profoundly difficult time in my life started to get to be too much, he reminded me that he Loved me and that I saved his life, by crawling up on my lap, resting his head on my chest, and looking up at me and purring until he fell asleep. I have had days when I didn't give either dog as much attention as they deserve, and days when I lost my temper, or got frustrated. But I did spend a lot of time teaching Spike to handle living in a new home, being groomed, examined on a table, and learning to accept his new family. It was worth every second. I wish I had done even more, and been more consistent, but looking back and realizing I helped a dog with an extremely hard life learn to be a happy member of our home while I was suffering from depression is something I am extremely proud of. I look back and remember very clearly how hard it was, how stressful it was for me and for Spike. I think about that often when he's sleeping on my lap or gazing up at me Lovingly while I'm working or watching TV. It was stressful and nerve-racking at times, but it was also incredibly rewarding. He had a date to be euthanized before we took him in. He was at death's door, and I think he knows we saved him. He still seems incredibly grateful. He is probably the most affectionate dog I've ever lived with. When I take a moment to stop and really appreciate everything Spike and I have been through together, from the first meeting at the shelter when he was awaiting his euthanasia date to watching him sleep at my feet right now as I type this, it literally takes my breath away. I just gasped out loud watching him sleep.

I didn't have time to get back to this book for many, many months and was feeling very discouraged about that. I did eventually try to get back to the book and finish it, but I could not. There were even days when I wasn't sure I believed in any of it anymore. I felt a little broken. Spike was a joy to have around, but still a lot of work, and could still be reactive around strangers. All the other problems with the pandemic and politics were still there, and the trauma of our plumbing nightmare was still fresh.

I have been feeling better lately. I have healthier sleep habits now. My partner and I have both received our first vaccination. Our toilet works beautifully. I decided to go back to the book a few days ago. My computer froze every time I tried to edit the text. I lost about a page of new material. I spent several hours trying different things, getting advice on community forums, looking up solutions on Google and FAQ pages. Nothing worked. I finally was able to do a live screen share with a tech support person, and they struggled with it for over an hour, having no more luck than I did. At one point, after confidently announcing they'd solved the problem only to find they had not, they just typed "wow" in the chat box. Eventually, they did get it working correctly. I was too frustrated to keep working on it and decided to leave it for the next morning. The next morning it froze again. I wasted another morning trying to fix it and had to do another screen-sharing session with a tech support agent that again dragged on for over an hour. This time, it was finally fixed properly and is now working normally. It was all very frustrating and worrying. While I was trying to solve the problem, I was worried that this would be the last straw, and that I would have to give up on the book. I was again starting to have doubts as to whether I believed in the things I was trying to write. It's 24 hours later as I am writing this, and I am a little surprised by how good I feel. It's been a challenging 48 hours, but I did my best, and things are OK. I am OK. I believe everything in this book is true, and I am back to work. Getting back to work on this book is healing for me, even when it's frustrating and hard. I struggled but I had enough fortitude to keep going. I had doubts, but I still had hope. I still believe Love is the most important thing in the world. I am not perfect, but I am good enough, and that cannot ever be taken away from me. I am committing to working on the book at least 30 minutes every morning and finishing the book by the end of summer. I'll let you know at the end of the book how that worked out.

Storytelling

When I work with a client, I don't just focus on stopping undesirable behavior. We identify problems we need to address, and we address them by figuring out what we want the dogs *to do*. We reward the things the dog can already do the way we want, and we build on those things. We also teach the dog new, desirable behaviors, so the dog knows what is expected, and can do that with confidence. We develop a training plan based on what we want to see happen, and work on daily exercises that get us closer to that goal. Having a training plan helps us focus on what we need *to do*, rather than obsessing over what has gone wrong in the past. This emphasis on encouraging and rewarding success is often a dramatic change in mindset for the clients. Instead of trying to make a bad dog submit, we focus on encouraging our dog to succeed. We change the story.

When we're looking at our own lives and identifying problems we want to address, we should address them by figuring out what we want *to do*. We need to set goals. We look at the things we are already doing that can get us closer to our goals and build on those things. We also try to figure out what other things we need to do to get us closer to our goals and work on them daily, just like with a training plan. With each successful step, we are writing a new chapter in the story of our lives.

      Stories, the ones we hear or read, and the ones we tell ourselves, are important. They're the inspiration and foundation of a training plan for our life, which is why most chapters in this book feature some of my favorite personal dog stories. Thinking of my life as a story or stories that I am telling myself helps me get focused, which isn't something that comes naturally to me. I have a little bit of a problem with ADD, and having a logically consistent story that I tell and re-tell myself every day helps a lot, maybe even more than ADD medication (which I sometimes forget to take because, duh). If the story we are telling ourselves is that we are bad, or screwed up, that is likely to be a self-fulfilling prophecy. Having a story that focuses on what we are doing right, and learning new, better habits, can only help. It is not a cure for every problem in your life. No story you tell yourself will ever cure you if you have a fatal disease or condition. Storytelling alone will not help you get over PTSD, depression, or anxiety disorders. There is no story you can tell yourself that will make you immune to violence and oppression. But looking at your life as an unpleasant story can only do harm. Sometimes we need to change the story. We need to find a good story in our lives. We need to celebrate the good we already do and work on the things we still need to do. Becoming a more virtuous person is the best possible way to do that. This book didn't cure the pandemic, it didn't fix my plumbing, it didn't cure my ADD, it didn't bring an end to political polarization, or make me immune to depression. But it did help me survive all those things when I was hurting. It helped me focus on my goals and the things I needed to do in methodical, measurable ways, and that helped me get back to telling the story I wanted to tell with this book and with my life. It is possible to take the math and science behind modern dog training and turn it into literature that can change the story of your dog's life, and yours too. I hope this book helps you find ways to tell stories that are happy and true.

Virtue

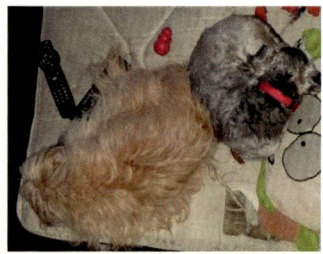

Virtue (Latin: *virtus*, Ancient Greek: ἀρετή *arete*) is moral excellence. A virtue is a trait or quality that is deemed to be morally good and thus is valued as a foundation of principle and good moral being. Personal virtues are characteristics valued as promoting collective and individual greatness.

When I am working with clients, I often tell them that keeping a close eye on body language, the dog's and our own, is extremely important, because it's the only language we can really share. We can teach a dog a lot of cue words, but they never really understand English, French, or any other language. They aren't going to write a play someday and we'll never have a conversation with them about philosophy, and that's OK. Most people don't write plays and many of us don't want to have lengthy conversations about philosophy either!

This first chapter deals with the philosophical approach to morality and ethics, and it is pretty nerdy. If you aren't interested in the details behind moral philosophy, feel free to skip this chapter. Everything I feel needs to be said can be found in the rest of this book. I included this chapter as a way of demonstrating that the ideas presented in this book are not my own. They are the product of centuries of careful thought by many people, most of whom are probably a lot smarter than I am. I minored in philosophy in college, and I am a nerd, so I enjoyed writing this chapter, but I won't be offended if you skip it.

Moral philosophy or ethics is usually divided into three subjects: metaethics, normative ethics, and applied ethics. Metaethics is concerned with the origins and meaning of ethics. The fact that much of what I intend to write about transcends individual cultures, has a scientific basis, was historically often discussed in religious contexts, and has its roots in ancient history, leads me to believe that there are eternal, moral truths, and that morality is something more than merely human convention. I don't claim to know where morality came from any more than I know where photosynthesis came from, so I am not going to spend a lot of time on metaethics, except to say that ethics or morality cannot possibly be something we just made up.

I will also be spending some time describing examples of these standards in action and how they can be applied, which is what applied ethics is concerned with. But this book is concerned primarily with normative ethics: Arriving at moral standards that regulate right and wrong conduct. Normative ethics can be divided into three types of theories: deontological theories, consequentialist theories, especially utilitarianism, and virtue theories. Deontological theories are rule- or duty-based. Immanuel Kant's categorical imperative is probably the most well-known deontological, rule-based approach to ethics, and is similar to the Golden Rule: "So act that you use humanity, whether in your own person or in the person of any other, always at the same time as an end, never merely as a means."[3] Consequentialist theories, not surprisingly, are focused entirely on the consequences of our actions. Utilitarianism is the most well-known consequentialist theory. It was first developed by Jeremy Bentham and can be summarized as follows: "The greatest happiness of the greatest number should be the guiding principle of conduct."[4] Virtue ethics is person-focused: it emphasizes the character of the individual person carrying out an action. All three of these approaches have value, so my approach to this is a mix of all three, but it's primarily aimed at virtue ethics: cultivating habits that produce a good character.

The Golden Rule is obviously a rule, and is therefore one possible example of a duty-based or deontological theory of ethics and is also central to this book and my understanding of morality and right conduct. But despite how simple it sounds, it's extremely difficult to apply. I do not believe it is humanly possible to follow the Golden Rule (treating everyone the way we would like to be treated: with dignity and respect) without spending a *lot* of time cultivating the habits that form good character and inspire right conduct. I also think that cultivating these virtues in a way that makes following the Golden Rule possible will result in "the greatest happiness for the greatest number," which is what the most well-known consequentialist theory, utilitarianism, advocates. All three approaches are appealing and helpful, but I think to follow the Golden Rule, and to create the circumstances for the greatest happiness for the greatest number, we *must* cultivate good character within ourselves. If we are merely following a rule, (duty theory of ethics) we will struggle *unless* that rule can be made second nature by cultivating our character and becoming more virtuous people. Consequentialist theories like utilitarianism will also cause us to struggle because the math isn't very easy to do, and there are consequences that are almost impossible to measure. Utilitarianism (even if they didn't call it utilitarianism) and an incomplete knowledge of reality is what led some people in ancient times to conclude human sacrifice was a good idea and morally sound. We still have an incomplete understanding of reality. We don't have enough information to do a precise cost/benefit analysis. We have no idea how much harm we do to ourselves when we look at other sentient beings that have just as much of a right to life, liberty, and happiness as we have, as if they were pieces of a math problem. If we look at another person and conclude that they create more unhappiness than happiness in the world, we must be prepared for the fact that they may be making a similar calculation about us. You can't follow the Golden Rule without cultivating your character first. You can't do the cost/benefit analysis consequentialists require with the limited amount of information individuals have. Even if you could, it would be very difficult to follow through without cultivating your character first in a way that makes good conduct habitual.

I've chosen the Golden Rule and the seven classic Christian virtues for my discussion of right conduct in this book. This is not the only way to frame virtues; other cultures in other parts of the world have all come up with equally satisfying and admirable descriptions, and I have learned to Love and admire many of them. But the seven Christian virtues, divided into the three theological virtues described by St. Paul in the 1st Letter to the Corinthians, (faith, hope, and Love) and the four cardinal virtues (prudence, justice, fortitude, and temperance) that we first encounter in Greek philosophers (Plato and Aristotle) have formed the foundation of my understanding of what it means to be a virtuous person.

You don't have to be a Christian to follow these virtues. Over half of them were developed before Christianity existed, and Christianity does not have an exclusive claim on faith, hope, and Love. Faith *does* seem to be a poisonous word to most atheists and agnostics, and I think they're right to be uncomfortable with it, which is why I used the word "trust" instead. Being trustworthy and seeking out trustworthy information seems far less problematic to me than "faith," which is why I am not using that word in this book. I'm not knocking faith; I think everyone has faith in some things they can't prove, and there is no need to pretend otherwise. But I think trust is a better thing to cultivate than faith.

In addition to cultivating the seven virtues, I think we need to cultivate a deeper appreciation for and understanding of math and science. We need to make sense of the physical world we live in, and math and science are the most objectively fair, reliable ways to do that. Science and math can't tell us how to be better, moral people, but they can help us understand our world and each other. We need that understanding if we are to make informed moral choices that cultivate the kind of character that we need to develop in ourselves, and to encourage in others.

I am taking it as an established fact that we have moral obligations to animals. Most scientists now believe all mammals, many birds, and possibly octopuses are all sentient. If they are sentient then, as Jeremy Bentham argued, the most important question is not how intelligent or powerful are they, but "Can they suffer?"[5] The answer to that question is a clear and unambiguous "Yes." If we are to consider ourselves moral beings, then any discussion about morality must include a discussion on our relationships with animals. As a dog trainer, I am keenly aware of the fact that respecting our dogs as sentient creatures to whom we have moral obligations not only makes logical, scientific sense, it works better than older dog-training models focusing on dominating or being the "alpha." This looks like a clear, scientific affirmation of the Golden Rule, one that includes *all* sentient creatures, including our beloved animal friends, and that's so beautiful that it thrills me.

For further reading: These are some of the sources I used for concepts and terms used in this chapter.
https://plato.stanford.edu/entries/ethics-virtue/
https://plato.stanford.edu/entries/moral-character/
https://iep.utm.edu/ethics/

Trust

One of the words I find myself using most often when dealing with clients is "trust." The first time I use it is in reference to the trainers and behaviorists that I admire and whose example I try to follow. I let clients know they can *trust* people like Ian Dunbar, Sophia Yin, and Patricia McConnell. They can trust them because they are proven experts who have spent their lives working with animals; they have the respect of their peers, they've all done groundbreaking research, and their work can get published in peer-reviewed academic journals.

There is a lot of contradictory advice out there on dog training. It can be hard to tell who is and who is not an expert if you aren't one yourself. You may have to do some research, and even then, there are no guarantees you will get it right. It's also possible for the experts you've identified to be wrong. Experts make mistakes too, but they are the ones who have done the most serious science, and they have earned our trust with decades of reliable research and a lifetime of hard work. Fortunately, canine behavioral experts *have* started to arrive at a clear consensus in recent years. The real, trustworthy experts are, for the most part, saying the same things. They all recognize that dogs learn by association and by trial and error (also called classical conditioning and operant conditioning), they all use reward-based training as their #1 tool, and they all reject the dominance theory approach you may have seen popularized on TV. Expert consensus can still be wrong of course: everyone is fallible and we're constantly learning. But a decades-long scientific consensus is going to be far more trustworthy than anything you see on a reality TV show or find with a quick Google search. You can trust science.

The second time I mention the word trust to clients is when they ask about punishment. Many people want to know if they should use a leash correction or some other physical punishment to let their dog know something they did was *wrong*. The answer is no, and the reason is trust. It's much harder to explain the reasons for punishment to a dog than it is to another human, making it very unlikely that your dog will understand that a leash correction, shock, or jab in the throat is "for their own good." You can tell them that, but they have no idea what those words mean. What the dog knows is you hurt or scared them when they did a particular act. That may make the dog less likely to engage in that same act in the future, but they will *not* learn the behavior was wrong; they will learn the behavior means *you* will hurt or frighten them. At that moment, they have started trusting you less. They may continue to suppress the unwanted behavior out of fear, but when the source of fear (you) is not around, the behavior is likely to return. Even worse, the dog may resort to a more extreme behavior instead; a dog that gets punished for barking at scary things will often decide biting scary things is a safer option.

Physically punishing children is controversial; most social scientists don't think it's a good idea. But you can explain, with precise language, why you are punishing the child, and what they can do to make sure they don't get punished again. We can't do that with our dogs, and as a result, dogs often misunderstand punishments. When we give our dogs an angry reprimand or harsh leash correction because they barked at another dog, they might learn that it happened because they barked, or they might learn that you frighten or hurt them when other dogs are nearby. This can cause their emotional response to get worse and could lead to even more aggressive behavior.

Dog training is completely unregulated, so there are a lot of voices out there promoting a lot of wildly contradictory ideas. You can't trust them all. At least one former TV dog training host used to advocate pinning your dog to the ground by force until they stop struggling as a way to "show them who's boss." This is violence, and I have seen this kind of behavior damage a dog and shatter their trust. One of the rescue dogs I've worked with is an adorable Shih Tzu named Springsteen. We don't know too much about his history, but there were some clues, including but not limited to his reactivity, that led me to suspect he may have been abused. His adopted family put in a lot of work to ease his fears, make his walks a little calmer and happier, and to earn his trust. He did learn to trust, and even Love them, and they Loved him back! His bite inhibition wasn't great, so they needed to be careful and monitor his body language closely, and respect his warning signs, and they usually did. One day on a walk, a neighbor asked how Springsteen was doing, and the dog, who was more reactive towards men than women, barked at him. The man grabbed Springsteen by the neck, slammed him to the ground and pinned him with his full body weight on the dog. "You gotta show 'em who's boss," he told them. After a few seconds of this violent assault, and that is exactly what it was, the owner insisted the man stop. Springsteen's mom took him home, and Springsteen hid and avoided them for days. Springsteen's mom wasn't going to be able to physically confront and stop the man that attacked her adopted baby, but Springsteen's trust issues with humans returned, and he no longer felt he could trust his family to keep him safe. I stopped by to help them get Springsteen trusting them again. It was incredibly sad and depressing to see this poor little dog, who had only just recently learned to start trusting people, cowering in fear after an attack. This horrible incident illustrated that even if you are interacting with your dog in a trustworthy, trust-building way, someone else can shatter that trust. Fortunately, most of our neighbors are unlikely to attack our dogs on walks, but other dog care professionals might, and many of them *do*. I have seen some very rough behavior, including "alpha rolls" like the one Springsteen was subjected to, inflicted on dogs by groomers, trainers, and day care attendants. It's important that you spend some time finding professional people that understand classical and operant conditioning, refuse to use pain or fear as training tools, and will earn your trust and your dog's. I am happy to report that while my friend Springsteen still has his unpredictable moments, he's happy again. His family was able to earn his trust back with patience and science-backed training methods.

If you give a dog a click with a clicker and a treat every single time they engage in a particular desirable behavior, like looking politely at a dog off in the distance and then looking at you, they *will* engage in that behavior more often. Think of the click as a promise that a well-earned reward will immediately follow. If you keep that promise every single time, you will have earned your dog's trust. This is how I taught our adopted dog Spike to accept Jeff. Every time he looked at Jeff, I marked the look with a click or the word "YES!" and immediately followed with a high value treat before any barking or lunging occurred. Eventually, Jeff stopped being scary, and became a treat-predicting machine in Spike's eyes. Spike soon realized that in addition to being a treat predicting machine, Jeff has a warm lap that he can sit on, and that Jeff is a reliable source of verbal praise and affection. He went from biting a stranger out of fear, to seeing that same stranger as a beloved family member in a matter of weeks. It's been well over a year and a half, and they adore each other. They trust each other.

I think we all tend to spend a little too much time doubting the trustworthiness of others, our dogs, other people's dogs, other dog owners, trainers, and even science. I'm not suggesting you start trusting everyone, all the time; that would be disastrous. No one wants to get taken in by a scam; no one wants to get burned. But there are a lot of people out there doing hard science and dedicating their lives to advancing our knowledge and understanding of dogs, and that kind of work deserves our respect and trust.

After we have identified legitimate, trustworthy experts, we don't need to spend a lot of time pointing out who is not trustworthy, and we probably shouldn't. Sometimes non-experts benefit from having their errors proven wrong because it gives them extra attention. People also often get defensive when their errors are pointed out, and their views can become hardened, especially if we're unpleasant or judgmental. Instead, we should concentrate on making ourselves more trustworthy. I am reminded of a famous biblical quote: "Why do you notice the splinter in your neighbor's eye, and not the beam in your own eye? Remove the beam from your own eye first, and then you will be able to see more clearly and remove the splinter from your neighbor's eye." (Matthew 7:3-5.) Instead of attacking other people for their trust issues, we should all work a little harder at fostering trust in ourselves and those around us.

You can earn your dog's Love and trust by refusing to engage in behaviors that might shatter that trust, like using fearful or painful tools on your dog as discipline, and by learning about reward-based training instead. You can earn the trust of your neighbors by teaching your dog polite greetings and calm behaviors. You can earn the trust of your fellow dog owners by refusing to judge them if you see them struggle. Finally, you can compliment trustworthy behavior whenever you see it. One of the lines I use most often with clients is: "Praise costs nothing, has zero calories, and we never run out, so we can be super generous with praise!" If there is one thing that positive reinforcement training has taught me it's this: Recognizing and rewarding trustworthy behavior produces more trustworthy behavior in others and in yourself.

Hope

Hope: A desire of some good, accompanied with an expectation of obtaining it, or a belief that it is obtainable; an expectation of something which is thought to be desirable; confidence; pleasing expectancy.

—*Webster's Revised Unabridged Dictionary*, 1913.

In the previous chapter I spoke about the importance of trust. I mentioned several of my dog-training heroes and noted that they have earned our trust with years of reliable scientific research. I also mentioned how important it is for people to earn their dog's trust. Having trustworthy information and being a trustworthy person are both important and they will make achieving your goals easier. But it's not enough. We all struggle sometimes; we all experience fear and self-doubt. Trusting that you have accurate information isn't going to help if you are paralyzed with feelings of fear or hopelessness. We need hope.

When I first started studying to become a dog trainer, I almost lost hope. About a half dozen times. I began my dog-training education in the Karen Pryor Academy, which runs the most successful professional dog-trainer class in the world. Two weeks before our final exam in the Dog Trainer Professional Class, my beloved dog

Buffy, for no obvious reason, stopped doing half of the behaviors she had learned. I was on the verge of panic. Eventually we figured out that she was suffering from joint pain; all the behaviors she was refusing involved moving her front legs. She didn't limp or show obvious signs of pain; she was being very stoic. Had I used punishment to force her to fight through the pain, I would have done permanent damage to her emotional state and to our relationship. Fortunately, my teacher Steve knew better. Buffy got some pain medication, and we were able to get back to work, but we lost a week of practice just before our final exam. Our final exam included a ten-part behavior chain that we had to cue our dog through. The day before the exam we were close but had still not yet gotten through the chain perfectly even one time. I wasn't certain she would be able to do it, but I knew she was close, and steadily getting closer. I was a little anxious, but I was also feeling hopeful again. The day of the exam I did have to re-cue *one* behavior, but other than that, she was perfect. That was her best run up to that point, and she did it far away from home under stressful conditions. The instructor was stunned and told the entire class about our struggles and even added "I honestly did not believe that was *possible*." After we finished, I went through the chain a few more times at home and she nailed it each time. I was so proud of her, and myself too. We both worked hard and did well.

I also started to lose hope at a recent Tricks Dog Instructor weekend workshop. I had borrowed a friend's dog for this workshop, and I underestimated how stressful this experience might be for him, and at first I handled it poorly. My own stress levels shot up and made things harder for the dog than it should have been. I did better as the day went on, but I was a mess all morning on day one. When I got home, I remember being a little disappointed with myself, but mostly I was determined *not* to repeat my mistakes the next day. If you've ever worked with me before, you've probably heard me recommend something called "The Jolly Routine," (a term coined by renowned canine behaviorist William E. Campbell).[6] It's a method for dealing with a dog who is stressed that is more effective than most of our attempts to be soothing. Oftentimes, clients will try to soothe their anxious dogs by saying, "There, there, it's OK," but dogs have *no* idea what those words mean. Even worse, many dogs will hear those words in stressful contexts often enough to actually start to see them as a predictor that scary things are coming. The Jolly Routine avoids these mistakes that most people, including me, often make. It teaches us to make the dog think it's party time and act silly and "jolly" instead. I reminded myself to take my own advice and use the Jolly Routine. I had seen it work before with other dogs, including this particular dog, so I knew it was a reliable technique that I could trust.

I was feeling confident when I went to bed that night. I told my spouse that I was feeling more confident and that things would go better the next day. When he asked, "How do you know?" I replied, "Because I know what I'm doing. I know what I did wrong, and I know how to fix it." The next day our teacher (Kyra Sundance) spoke about the importance of using your "happy voice" when training. She looked right at me when she said it and then added, "Right, Daniel?" so I laughed a little and said, "I'm doing much better today!" She said it playfully, not rudely, and I appreciated it. More importantly, I *did* do better that day, a *lot* better! In fact, not to brag, but I rocked on day two. I was calm and confident, my timing and technique improved, and I felt like a different person. I didn't do it on my own. My canine buddy Bernie was performing like a star now that I had changed my own attitude, and I was pretty impressed with how well he handled himself considering I made day one a lot more stressful than it needed to be. We finished the workshop together and had a great time. We turned into a good team.

Some people may be surprised to hear me talk about getting discouraged or starting to lose hope. I don't think that's how I usually appear to other people. I am not a particularly anxious person, I never panic, I rarely lose my temper, and I almost never feel hopeless. But everyone struggles sometimes; no one is immune. We've all failed before. We all make mistakes; we all experience doubt and fear. Hope is the antidote for our doubt and fear. That's why hope, unlike other positive emotions, appears when things are not going so well. Writing for *Psychology Today*, Dr. Barbara Fredrickson explains hope this way:

> [Hope] removes the blinders of fear and despair and allows us to see the big picture. We become creative, unleashing our dreams for the future. This is because deep within the core of hope is the belief that things can change. No matter how awful or uncertain they are at the moment, things can turn out for the better. Possibilities exist. Belief in this better future sustains us.[7]

Modern, science-based dog training can help you focus on the pursuit of excellence, even when you are struggling with self-doubt. We're taught to set ourselves and our dogs up for success. We set a simple, easily achievable goal, and then build on it. We don't expect that our dog will learn to do something complicated like slamming cupboard doors closed on command or finding a hidden container filled with wintergreen odor in a crowded room or on a car in one session. We break it down into many simple, achievable steps. As soon as we get the first simple step done, we pat ourselves on the back (and our dogs!) as a reward for a job well done. Then we work on the next step, and the next, and so on. If you get stuck, just go back to an easier step so you can experience some success again and then start raising criteria, more gradually this time, based on what you've learned. As your dog succeeds and gets rewarded by you, you will also get rewarded by your dog! Your dog will classically and operantly condition you to Love training with them, because they will have fun, and you Love seeing your dog happy! That's classical conditioning. Soon you'll start making choices that increase your dog's happiness more often. That's operant conditioning. With each successful step, you and your dog will feel more confident and hopeful.

This isn't simply a good way to train your dog; it's a good way to live your life. Learning the value of tracking progress and rewarding myself for that progress made me a better dog trainer. It also made me a better dart player. After having some success tracking progress with my dog, I started writing down my scores when I practiced darts and tracking my dart-practice progress. I am now a better dart player as a result, and I need that, because darts is a game specifically designed to crush your hopes! The biggest targets on the board (20, 19, 18, 17) are bracketed on either side by the smallest numbers (1, 2, 3, 4, 5). You can be just a hair away from a triple 20 three times in a row and end up with just three points. That's disheartening. But if you keep getting better, eventually you'll start hitting twenties and even triple twenties with some degree of regularity. You can feel the hope dispelling your fears of failure when that's happening.

Modern dog trainers always ask: "What do you want your dog *to do*?" People will often say "To stop pulling," or "To stop barking!" and we will respond with "But what do you want them to *do*?" It's easy to get so focused on stopping undesirable behavior that we forget that it's even more important to teach the dog what we want them to do. We can suppress a bark or stop pulling with punishment, but that's not the best way to address these problems. A better mindset is to figure out specifically what we *want* the dog to do instead like, "Walk calmly by my side," or, "Greet guests with all four paws on the floor," for example. If we have a clear goal like, "I want my dog to walk calmly by my side," and we rely on trustworthy people using proven methods as our guide and put in the time and work in a way that earns our dog's trust, our odds of success will be extremely high. We have a realistic expectation of a good, desirable outcome, and trustworthy methods to make that outcome happen, and these two things combined generate a "pleasing expectancy," and this pleasing expectancy we have created within ourselves is *hope*.

"Pleasing expectancy" is the definition of hope I like best from Webster's. It's not always easy to expect a pleasing result. You are going to struggle with your dog, and you are going to mess up sometimes. There's a chance that something you want to do won't work out, and you might fail. I didn't write about any of my failures in this chapter, but I have had more than my share. I have failed hard at things that were important to me many times, just like everyone else. That's OK. You don't need to succeed at everything you do; that's not even possible. You need to be reasonable in your goal setting. If you have a reasonable goal, and you are using trustworthy, reliable methods to achieve those goals, and if you don't give up, your odds of success are going to be high, and your success will make it easier to hope in the future.

There are a lot of things that can go wrong, and there will be some disappointments, so we need to learn to be patient. As I mentioned in the "Trust" chapter, sometimes it can be hard to find qualified experts that provide reliable information. It's tempting to cut corners, set unrealistic goals, push things too fast; it's easy to make mistakes. If you suffer from clinical depression or anxiety, this can be especially difficult, and you may need help from your doctor. But science, trustworthy information, cultivating trustworthiness in yourself, and steady methodical work will produce good results and, just as importantly, these things can give you hope, even when you are struggling with fear and self-doubt.

Love

Love is patient, Love is kind.
It does not envy, it does not boast,
it is not proud.
It is not rude, it is not self-seeking,
it is not easily angered,
it keeps no record of wrongs.
Love does not delight in evil
but rejoices with the truth.
It always protects, always trusts,
always hopes, always perseveres.
Love never fails.

—1 Corinthians 13:4-8, NIV

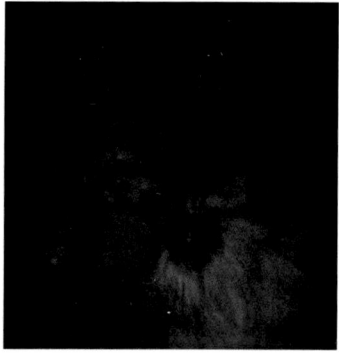

The passage above is from Paul's Letter to the Corinthians, chapter 13. St. Paul's description of Love is one of the most beautiful things I've ever read. It's one of the most famous passages in the Bible and is still frequently used in weddings. Later in the same chapter Paul adds, "And now faith, hope, and Love abide, these three; *and the greatest of these is Love.*" (1 Corinthians 13:13, NRSV.) I could not possibly agree with Paul more when he says: "*The greatest of these is Love.*"

Paul is not referring to romantic Love here. That's one of two common misunderstandings people have about this passage. He's referring to *agape* (Ancient Greek:

ἀγάπη): the selfless, unconditional, parental Love God has for us, and the Love we return to God. C. S. Lewis defined *agape* as a Love that is "*wholly disinterested and desires what is simply best for the beloved*,"[8] and believed it to be the highest level of Love known to humanity. I think I like that definition best, and that is what I am referring to when I talk about Love in this book. The other thing people often misunderstand about this passage is that it's one of the Bible's pleasant, easier teachings. There is nothing easy about this understanding of Love. It's an incredibly high standard of behavior and a serious commitment. Love, understood this way, may begin as a feeling, or it may cause feelings to develop, but it isn't just a feeling; it's also work. We can't possibly have passionate Love for every single individual on earth, but we can have a passionate Love for our commitment to the well being of others. In this sense, it's possible to Love someone you don't even like, if you are passionately committed to their well-being. That passionate commitment to another's well-being can sometimes inspire feelings of Love. The Christian New Testament teaches that "God *is* Love." (1 John 4:8.)

Love is the foundation that all the other virtues rely on. This description of Love from Paul mentions at least two of the virtues (trust and hope), and lists qualities associated with the other virtues, like patience, perseverance (fortitude), humility (temperance), protection (justice). Surprisingly, this passage also sounds a lot like modern, science-based dog training to me: patient, kind, humble, empathetic, not easily angered, not punishing when they get something wrong, always persevering, trusting and hopeful. This is what Love is, and it's exactly how I was taught to work with dogs. It's the reason I Love my job as much as I do.

The Beatles, the first musical act I ever fell in Love with, had a famous song called, "All you need is Love." As much as I Love the Beatles, I'm not willing to go quite that far. I do think Love is the most important thing in our lives. But we also need the most reliable, trustworthy information we can find, we need to be as honest with each other and ourselves as possible, and we need to find reasons to hope when we are in danger of giving in to doubt or fear. But Love is what inspires us to do the work needed to find trustworthy information, and to find reasons to hope. Love is what inspires us to get help when our behavior is hurting people we care about. Love is what gives our lives meaning. Love is not the only thing we need, but it is the thing we need the most.

As a Karen Pryor Academy Certified Training Partner (KPA CTP) who has also been Low Stress Handling Certified (LSH Silver), Fear Free certified, and has worked with dogs for many years, I have access to a lot of trustworthy information. But even with all that information at my disposal, and the years of experience I have had working with dogs, I can think of at least two people who have done far more than I have to help dogs, without any of the formal training or professional experience that I have: Carly and Tina. They both run rescue agencies; one is called Coveted Canines and the other is Boston Terrier Network Canada. Together they have saved the lives of thousands of dogs, helping thousands of families add a new furbaby to their Loving homes. Knowing that you saved a life and helped a Loving family grow and widen the circle of Love in their home is one of the most rewarding things you can do. I've been a part of that process for many families, but not as many as Tina and Carly. They work very hard at it, and it's all done out of Love. They genuinely Love the dogs and people they help. They still often need to refer to professional trainers for assistance and are smart enough and humble enough to do that without hesitation.

Volunteering for rescue agencies has been one of the most rewarding experiences of my life. Most rescues are volunteer driven, and most of the people I've volunteered with do it out of Love for, and a desire to save, dogs. One of the dogs I met while volunteering for Coveted Canines was a little guy whose name was Harry, but he didn't know that. I'm not sure he even knew the word "sit" when I met him. One of the foster managers that had met Harry asked me to meet him and do an assessment. She wanted to help but wasn't sure if we had anyone that could handle fostering Harry.

Harry was at death's door. Physically he was healthy, but he was untrained, fear aggressive, loud, and kind of wild. No one had applied to adopt him, and he'd been in the shelter for six months. He was a street dog before that. When I met him, a shelter employee was trying to leash him up with a slip lead and was really struggling. He was using a slip lead because it's secure, not as a punishing training tool, but he couldn't get it on because Harry was biting at it. I'm pretty sure he was trying to play with it at first, because the man was trying to sort of lasso him into it, and Harry Loved rope toys, so he jumped and bit at the leash for fun. Unfortunately, the human was getting increasingly frustrated, which was causing Harry to get frustrated and eventually angry. I offered to put the leash on by just luring him through it. I normally do not recommend luring a dog through something scary because it can cause the dog to stop trusting you and even fear the lure. But Harry wasn't afraid of the leash; he thought it was a toy. I wasn't too worried about luring him into a leash under the circumstances, and his Love for going outside would make fading the lure out easy. Harry was very happy to accept the leash, even though he had no idea how to walk politely while on it. I let him run as soon as we got to the fenced-in back yard and he had a massive amount of energy. He Loved to run, he Loved to chase balls, he Loved to play tug, and he Loved sitting on my lap. He almost seemed to be looking for my approval. Every time he whipped a rope toy around or caught a ball, he'd turn and happily look at me, almost as if to say, "See how much fun I am? Don't you want to play with me?" I did want to play with him, and it was a lot of fun!

He didn't know how to behave politely, however. At one point after fetching a ball, he came running at me full speed, and as I knelt to say hi, he launched himself at my face and hit me in the nose with his head. He made my eyes water, he slammed into me so hard! It was pure affection though. He wanted to be Loved very badly. He made these weird sounds that I initially thought were growls, but happened when his body language was loose, wiggly, and happy. We eventually realized it was like purring, groaning, or sighing with happiness. I think we kind of fell in Love with each other that first meeting. The shelter asked if I thought our rescue had anyone that could foster him, and I said, "Definitely. I want to foster him. And maybe adopt him too. Haven't mentioned fostering to the spouse yet, but we'll see what he has to say. I'll come back with our dog next week to see if they get along." I came back with Buffy, and they got along fine. They even played a little, and Buffy hardly ever played with other dogs at that point in her life. She liked other dogs and was happy to greet them with a polite butt sniff, but rarely played with them.

Harry was a massive amount of work. He didn't know any basic commands, had a lot of fear aggression, especially when being handled, wasn't house trained, could be a resource guarder, had separation anxiety, and needed medication for anxiety. He kept me up all night multiple nights in a row. He bit my husband's hand the very first time he met him. He had no idea what his name was, so we changed it to Spike, after a character from Buffy the Vampire Slayer. Now Buffy and Spike are family, and we Love them both. Spike hit me in the nose with his head the day he met me, and bit Jeff the day he met him. He was a ton of work. It took a lot of patience, kindness, understanding, and effort. I would not have been able to do it, especially this past year, without a lot of Love. Fortunately, Love is a renewable resource: the more you give, the more you get. Spike is grateful to be part of our lives and Loves us very much, and we feel the exact same way about him.

I could have dealt with his problematic behaviors forcefully, or angrily or even, as some would say, in a "calm-assertive" way. He did not need someone to be assertive with him, calm or not. He needed someone to have some patience, and earn his trust, and to Love him. When people tell me positive reinforcement training doesn't work with difficult dogs, I mention scientific studies that have proven this to be false. I also mention my newest family member, Spike. He's not perfect, but that's OK; neither am I, and I've been told I'm delightful! (I have *really* nice friends that say really nice things.)

The slogan for my business is, "Treating every client, canine and human, the way we would like to be treated, with dignity and respect." This is a rewording of the Golden Rule: Do unto others as you would do have them do unto you. Another way to say (essentially) the same thing is the great Immanuel Kant's categorical imperative: "Treat every rational entity as an end in itself, and not as a means to an end." Every culture on earth has some version of the Golden Rule, and many of our most brilliant philosophers, like Kant and John Rawls, advocate a similar principle. It unites philosophy, religious traditions, and modern, science-based dog training.

Even though science, philosophy, and our cultural traditions all agree that treating each other with the same dignity and respect we desire is correct, we often don't. I trust the science and philosophy that confirms the Golden Rule. I have hope that we will all one day learn to treat each other, our animals, our fellow people, even our

45

enemies, with the same Love and respect that we all know we should. But we aren't there yet; we fail to live up to this standard often. Even +R (positive reinforcement) dog trainers fail. We are people that preach, "Don't focus on what's wrong, reward what is right and build on it," "Aversives are problematic," "It's just behavior, don't judge." But try to square that with the angry, judgmental, and very aversive denunciations of Cesar Millan that +R trainers make all the time. I think most of us try to be fair most of the time, but I often read comments from positive reinforcement trainers that sound vicious, even hateful. I feel certain Cesar Millan's approach to dog training is wrong, but I don't hate him, and I'm not going to judge him. I know how easy being wrong is; I've got plenty of experience being wrong. We've all got plenty of experience being wrong. We're all fallible. Most of us are wrong about a half a dozen different things before we eat breakfast. While I do think people who use outdated training methods are wrong, that does not mean they are bad people, or that they don't Love dogs. I will not judge them. I can discuss different training methods with different people and feel comfortable being critical of bad ideas, but we should take the same attitude towards people that get something wrong as we do towards dogs that get something wrong: Be patient, don't get angry, don't use violence, don't accidentally reward the wrong behavior in some way, and make sure that you reward good behavior often. *"Love is patient, Love is kind, it is not easily angered, it keeps no record of wrongs."*

We have learned to Love dogs that engage in inappropriate behavior or seem to struggle with simple cued behaviors. We don't judge them. We try not to get angry with them. We patiently try to help them because we Love them.

This approach has been spreading succesfully all over the world. Aidan Bindoff has a quote I Love on the

KPA web page about "never ever behaviors," a term coined by some trainers in a Yahoo group: "*Given enough thought, creativity, time, and, of course, clicker training, the 'never ever' behavior becomes a 'must do' challenge. The funny thing is, they almost always end up being achieved!*"[9] I Love that quote, but I would amend it slightly: "Given enough thought, creativity, time, clicker training and, of course, Love, the 'never ever' behavior becomes a 'must do' challenge that almost always ends up being achieved." Many years ago, animal trainer Keller Breland said, "I can train *any* behavior that the animal is physically and mentally capable of doing."[10]

We can accomplish seemingly impossible things while teaching animals like dogs and cats with trusted scientific methods and Love. Imagine what kind of world we can all create together if our interactions with each other were guided by science and motivated by Love. With enough "thought, creativity, time" and Love, we could *literally do **anything***. There *are no limits* if we try to teach and learn from each other this way: with patience, kindness, humility, trust, hope, and Love. And the greatest of these is Love.

Justice

1. *the maintenance or administration of what is just especially by the impartial adjustment of conflicting claims or the assignment of merited rewards or punishments*
2. *the quality of being just, impartial, or fair*
3. *conformity to truth, fact, or reason*

—Merriam-Webster, https://www.merriam-webster.com/dictionary/justice.)

I've been dog-obsessed for years, so some people may not know that my degree is actually in political science. When studying poli-sci, I discovered the writings of the legendary political philosopher John Rawls, author of *Justice as Fairness* (2001), one of my all-time favorite book titles! Rawls argued that we should imagine ourselves setting up a new society without any idea what our eventual position in that society will be and, from this original position behind a veil of ignorance, we are to devise a civilization that is equally fair to everyone. The idea is that if we look at things from this perspective, we will most likely envision a society in which people have a chance to be rewarded for exceptional efforts, but also one in which even the most vulnerable people have a chance to succeed and lead a whole, fulfilling life, in a society that is fair for everyone.

When you think about this thought experiment, it's clear that what Rawls has envisioned is a society based on the Golden Rule. Everyone is *not* to think merely of their own personal wants, but to make sure *everyone* gets a *fair* chance, that suffering is minimized, and that everyone is treated with the same dignity and respect that we wish to be treated with.

Like the Golden Rule and Immanuel Kant's categorical imperative, Rawls's ideas are part of the deontological (duty- or rule-based theory of ethics) model rather than the virtue-based model I am promoting in this book. But the rule/duty approach advocated by Rawls and Kant, along with the consequentialist approach found in Jeremy Bentham's utilitarianism, can help inform and improve our virtue-based approach. Following John Rawls's ideas on justice as fairness will improve our relationships with our dogs, and we will be rewarded by our dogs for treating them fairly. If we continue to work at being fairer, we will not only improve our relationships with our dogs, we will treat other people better and improve our relationships with them as well. John Rawls was promoting his theory of justice as a duty we should follow. It will be easier to do that if we try to cultivate the habit of justice as a virtue in ourselves.

For a lot of people justice means making sure bad behavior gets *punished.* Those people are what I like to call "Wrong!" Justice to me is more about making sure people get rewarded for their efforts, that they do not suffer unnecessary harm, and that we are fair in our dealings with each other. Punishment is, to me, the least essential element of justice. Some punishments are fair. If your dog is pulling frantically to get to a pee-stained fire hydrant or the dog park and yanking you off your feet, it's fair not to allow yourself to be dragged and insist that your dog walk politely before allowing them to enjoy the fire hydrant or their friends. When you stop because they're pulling, that *is* a punishment to the dog. But it's not a punishment that will hurt them or frighten them, and it will not make them trust you less. When you try to get a dog to walk politely by your side and give them a treat for doing so, that's justice. That's *fair*. You asked for a specific behavior that may not be what the dog had in mind, but they did what you wanted, and you gave them what they wanted. That's fair. That's justice.

A common complaint I hear in response to this is: "I don't want my dog to do what I say just because I give him treats! I want him to do it out of Love!" Why not flip that question and look at it from your dog's point of view? "I don't want him to give me a treat because I am walking like a soldier following orders, I want him to give me a treat because he *Loves* me!" Many people wonder if their dogs *really Love them* because the dogs don't always obey. What they are tragically missing is the dog may be wondering the same thing: "Do they *really Love me*? They know I Love freeze-dried liver, but they refuse to give it to me even when I am hungry and *begging!*"

A lot of trainers justify treat rewards as payment for a job well done, and that's a very good analogy: They did what they were told to do and have earned some pay/treats. But a job isn't really my favorite analogy for training, even though it does have some value and I do use it from time to time. The problem with it is that most people don't Love their boss. Doing things for pay is not enough by itself. A happy and fulfilling life involves more than getting paid to do your job. Sometimes what you need is not cash, but a hug, or some help moving, or hearing someone say, "I Love you." That's why we also give our dogs verbal praise, play, exercise, mental stimulation, and our attention and affection. We do *all* these things because we Love them, and because we know that they will do all the things that show they Love *us*: wagging tails, play, snuggles, and their attention and affection.

Our relationship with our dogs is not a master/slave relationship, it's not based on dominance/submission, it's not even really a pack leader/follower relationship, and it's more than a job. It's family. Seeing our relationship with our dogs in any other way is, in my view, unfair, and therefore unjust.

We ask an awful lot of our dogs. We expect them to suppress many normal, natural behaviors. We want them to do things that don't come naturally to them like sitting quietly even when all alone for many hours, or accepting the approach of strangers, even rude ones, or stopping play whenever we tell them to, not when they think they're done, or giving up objects that they thought were theirs because they found them fair and square, or knowing that the soft porous spot in the grass is *good* for going potty, but the soft, porous spot on the rug is *not.* We ask *all* of this of a creature that has a fraction of our intelligence, one that cannot understand our language beyond a handful of words, and does not even share compatible DNA with us. As Spider-Man's Uncle Ben once said, "With great power comes great responsibility." In any relationship, the one with more power has more responsibility. We have *a lot* of power over our dogs, even if it doesn't always feel that way. We control their access to food, water, shelter, and social experiences. We're bigger, stronger, and smarter. If there is a problem in our relationship with our dog, *we* are the ones with the responsibility to figure out a solution, not the dog, because we are the ones with all the power in that relationship, and we are the ones best equipped to solve those problems. Abusing the power advantage we have is not only unfair and harmful to the abused party, it's harmful to the abuser as well.

When I was taking my Karen Pryor Academy Dog trainer professional course, I remember seeing a list called "The Problem with Punishment," and one of the items on the list was "Punishment is reinforcing to the punisher," and it seemed to imply that the use of punishment can be rewarding to the punisher. The first example of this that comes to mind is what's called the "torturer's high." I don't think this is what motivates most punishment-based dog training though. Most punishment-based trainers believe their methods work better. The science may show that they're wrong, but they aren't crazy or cruel for believing their methods are better. Most of us that follow the latest scientific standards did not when we started out, so we should try to be a little more understanding towards people making the exact same mistakes we did. Punishment can sometimes suppress undesirable behavior quickly, but it risks damaging the dog's emotional state and causing them to trust you less.

People can also be tricked into believing punishment works better than rewards by something called "regression to the mean." I've seen this phenomenon described in multiple places, most recently in an article by Kayla Fratt from JourneyDogTraining.com, while discussing a book called *Thinking Fast and Slow* by Daniel Kahneman.[11] The case studied in this book involved Israeli fighter pilots and the use of rewards/punishments to improve performance. Researchers told the instructors that they would get better results rewarding good performances, but instructors reported back that they got better results with punishment. The reason for this is "regression to the mean." This can be a little hard to understand, but the key point is that exceptional performances, good or bad, are relatively rare, and will therefore usually be followed by average ones. In this case study, an exceptionally good performance tended to occur, on average, just one time out of ten, and an exceptionally poor performance also tended to occur about one time out of ten. This means that either an exceptionally good performance, or an exceptionally bad one, is likely to be followed by an average one. If you punish an exceptionally bad performance, the next one is likely to be better because average performances happen most of the time. This means you may think the punishment is what caused the improvement, and you will be reinforced for punishing. When the instructors reward an exceptionally good performance, an average or "mean" performance is likely to follow, and that will be a less impressive performance than the exceptionally good one you rewarded. This will make the instructor think that punishment works, and rewards do not. This is wrong. Long term trend lines make it very clear that people (and dogs!) tend to do better with rewards for good behavior. But "regression to the mean" and the inflated value we place on anecdotal data can make the opposite appear true.

This is why we should not be judging balanced and punishment-based trainers harshly. They are making a very common, understandable mistake. We all make mistakes every day, and we are probably not even aware of most of them. Over time, a reliance on punishment can become cruel. If the overall average does not improve, you are likely to punish more, because you thought it worked before and the learner is just being stubborn now. Eventually, over time, this can lead to serious abuse. In some extreme cases, it's torture. I have seen at least two trainers hang a dog in the air on a leash by its neck; once with a reality TV dog trainer, and once in person. That was torture, and it's not debatable. The heartbreaking thing about the trainer I personally witnessed do this is that he was, and is, a person I like and respect. He was convinced physical punishment was the way to train dogs and was doing his best, but he had to continually escalate, until he was literally torturing a dog. I am not proud to admit I waited too long to say anything, but I did eventually. To his credit, he admitted he went too far, appeared to be pained by what he did, and pledged never to do that again. He was an honorable person, but his reliance on physical punishment hurt him *and* the dog he was working with on that day. I want to make sure I am not slandering dog trainers who use methods I am uncomfortable with. Most of the ones I have met are animal Lovers who use what they sincerely believe to be the minimum physical punishment necessary to help the dog they are working with. They are not monsters and some of them do help a lot of people. But they are mistaken when they tell themselves they are using the minimum physical punishment. The smallest amount of physical punishment you *need* to use with 99% of dogs is none. When you allow yourself the option of using things like pain and fear as training tools, you are taking a risk with your dog and yourself that you do not need to take.

Far too many of us in the modern, science-based dog-training community are too quick to see those that use punishment as monsters. With a few exceptions, they are not. Some of them are very restrained in their use of punishment, have impeccable timing, and are honorable people. There are also a small number of cases out there in which expertly timed, measured punishments can help a dog that is struggling with positive methods. In the last five years, I have met, at most, just one dog that I believed could not be helped with purely positive methods. That dog also had a neurological condition and may not have been helped by *any* methods. But in some very, very rare cases, some dogs may need expertly applied, professional punishment for their rehabilitation. These dogs need to be referred to a professional, experienced, university-educated behaviorist, because they require a surgically precise degree of precision, skill, and timing. *Most* dog trainers lack the precision, skill, and timing to consistently apply punishments safely. I've *never* met a dog owner with that level of skill. Fortunately, for nearly every dog you meet, you don't need to use physical punishment. Thousands and thousands of trainers like me have been proving this for decades by refusing physical punishments and generously rewarding our dogs for cooperating with us.

If the dog cooperates with our solutions, which will probably come in the form of a training plan, then they must be rewarded in some way. Not rewarding a dog for going against his instincts at our command is fundamentally unjust. It's just not fair. Maybe you can get a dog to obey without any rewards, but if they do, it is either because they are scared, or because they are a nicer person than you are. It's equally unjust not to pay attention to *what* counts as a just reward for your dog. If your dog walks politely by your side and the only reward she ever gets is a pat on the head, she may not continue walking as politely as you like, because there is a good chance your dog does not see petting on the head as rewarding at all. Most dogs learn to tolerate it, and some Love it, but many others find it a little annoying. You need to find out what your dog *really* wants, and you must give them that when they do what *you* want, or you are just not being fair. The old, outdated dominance/submission model is not appropriate for your family, and your pet dog *is* part of your family. Studies of wolf packs have proven that the "alpha male" myth was never really correct. This fact has been confirmed by modern researchers, including the author of one of the most influential (and flawed) studies of wolf packs: David Mech. After observing wolves in a national park, Mech wrote a book (*The Wolf: The Ecology and Behavior of an Endangered Species*) in 1970 affirming the idea of the alpha male that had been popularized years before by studying captive wolves in a zoo. The widespread use of the terms "alpha male," "dominance," and "submission" can be traced to these studies. Mech and other researchers subsequently spent many years studying wolves in the wild and discovered real wolf packs do not function as dominant/submissive or master/underling relationships; they're family relationships. Mech's paper "Alpha status, dominance, and division of labor in wolf packs" was a major turning point in understanding the structure of wolf packs and has been repeatedly confirmed by later research.[12]

Dominance and submission are real words that describe real things, but they describe situational behaviors, not inflexible character traits. Some competent, modern trainers will use these words in certain situations, but in my experience it's almost never necessary. The pack leaders are mom and dad or grandma and grandpa. They are respected as the leaders because they fed and cared for their family, *not* because they dominated them. Real pack leaders in the wild can often be seen caring for the smaller, weaker, wolves, rather than dominating them. It is long past time we started treating dogs with the same dignity and respect that wolves treat their families with. I think we should be able to behave *at least* as virtuously and morally towards our family as a wolf living in the wild does to their family. We owe it to them.

"He is your friend, your partner, your defender, your dog. You are his life, his Love, his leader. He will be yours, faithful and true, to the last beat of his heart. You owe it to him to be worthy of such devotion." —Anonymous

Fortitude

[Bree and Hwin] were doing, if not all they could, all they thought they could, which is not quite the same thing.

—C. S. Lewis, *A Horse and His Boy*

The virtue of fortitude is strongly associated with courage, patience, and determination. I sometimes associate it with hope, because they're both things we need to get us through hard times. All the virtues are related to each other, they all complement each other, but they are all different. The "pleasing expectancy" I described when talking about hope is as much a feeling as a virtue, while fortitude is the strength of character you need to develop even when you are decidedly *not* pleased: when you are frightened, or angry, or exhausted. I mentioned in an earlier chapter that finding trustworthy information and being trustworthy yourself can help you create hope within yourself, but it's not always easy; it takes effort. It takes courage, patience, and determination. It takes fortitude.

We've all needed fortitude during the coronavirus pandemic. It's been a difficult time. Millions of people around the world have died and many more have become extremely sick. We haven't been able to go to restaurants, concerts, movies, or sporting events. We haven't been able to visit family as much as we'd like. I desperately miss hugs. Millions of people have lost their jobs. Every other problem we have in our society has been magnified by the pandemic: inequality, political polarization, poverty, and mental health problems. There have been times when I lost hope. Fortunately, I have been blessed with two perfect examples of fortitude to help me when hope is hard to come by.

My parents, Jean and Joe Josselyn, had hard lives. My mother was abused as a child by her stepfather. She almost died not long after I was born from an aortic aneurysm and lost the use of her hands, which she never got back. Her aorta seemed like it was trying to kill her for most of her life. She had multiple close calls, including an aortic dissection when she was an elderly woman, the same thing that killed a much younger John Ritter. She survived, but it damaged her voice and took most of her strength. She would never drive a car again after that and died of lung cancer six years later. She also had to suffer through my father's multiple, crippling anxiety disorders, which was not easy.

My father suffered from a severe case of general anxiety disorder, panic attacks, and agoraphobia. His agoraphobia was so bad that throughout my childhood I never even saw him sit inside a stationary car, even with the engine turned off. He worked at a store directly across the street from our home, so he didn't need to drive, but having two parents that could not drive was not always easy. Eventually, my mom found out about a knob you can attach to your steering wheel that she could manipulate to drive, and she got her license back. She was even eventually able to get my dad to go on short car rides to visit their kids or go out to eat. When she had her aortic dissection, she lost her license again, and that was heartbreaking. So, my dad, now an elderly man who *none* of us thought would ever get behind the wheel again, went out and got his license so he and my mom could still go places together. *That* is fortitude. He suffered from the worst case of agoraphobia I've ever seen, one that seemed impossible to conquer, until he did. He still had his limits, and he never got over it, but to see him fight off the worst part of his agoraphobia as an elderly man is an example of fortitude I will never forget. It gives me hope that maybe both of my parents passed some of their fortitude to me.

Hope did not come naturally to my dad. His panic attacks came often and every time they made him feel like he was going to die, and he was helpless to do anything about it. It's hard to imagine how awful that is. If you've ever had a moment where you genuinely feared you were going to die, then you know it's a terrifying feeling that you never forget. I have a vivid memory of being nearly hit by a car when I was a child, and it scared me so badly I started crying even though I was completely unhurt. I will never forget that moment of life-threatening panic. My dad had that feeling every single day. Some days he felt that way over and over again throughout the day. I still don't know how he was able to bear it, especially on top of all his other problems. But, my God, that man worked as hard as he could, long grueling hours for too little pay, and then did repairs on our cheap little home, and still found time to play football with us every Sunday.

When I was little, I was awestruck by my mother's patience. My dad panicked very easily and often, he could say foolish things, and he got on everyone's nerves with his constant anxiety, but my mom could always handle it somehow. Or at least that's what I always thought. Before she died, she admitted to me that she almost left him when I was in college, and I was surprised, but I understood. She did struggle to deal with his anxiety; it was a real hardship for her, and for the rest of us too. But it didn't hurt anyone as badly as it hurt him. He was not the most politically correct person I ever knew, and he would sometimes say things without thinking, but he beat himself up mercilessly for this. He believed he was stupid and frequently referred to himself as a dummy and never believed he was good enough. But he never let me feel that way about myself; he never let me doubt that I was Loved, or that I deserved to be. They were so different in so many ways, but the thing they shared was their Love and gratitude for us, their five kids. I spent my whole life knowing that the two most courageous and Loving people I'd ever known thought *I* was one of the five greatest things that had ever happened to them, and more than that, they made me believe I was one of the five greatest things that ever *could* have happened to them.

They suffered through physical and mental disabilities and illnesses, childhood trauma, poverty, and never seemed to catch a break. Yet they kept going, trying their best, working hard, and expressing gratitude for all the Love that they had in their lives. When my mother was being taken by helicopter to Mass General after her aortic dissection, with a 50/50 shot at surviving at best, I remember her taking my hand and telling me, "It's OK, I've had a wonderful life," and she smiled at me, and I knew she meant it. She thought she was going to die, but she didn't seem afraid, even though I know she must have been.

To me, despite their disabilities, they were both perfect. I have heard it said that the pursuit of excellence is inspiring, but the pursuit of perfection is discouraging. I Love that quote, because it reminds me that things don't always go the way they should; this is not a perfect world, but we can still strive for excellence. I don't Love it quite as much as I used to though, because there is another way of thinking about perfection that my parents lived out in their lives, from the movie *Friday Night Lights* (2004):

> To me, being perfect is not about that scoreboard out there. It's not about winning. It's about you and your

60

relationship with yourself, your family, and your friends. Being perfect is about being able to look your friends in the eye and know that you didn't let them down, because you told them the truth. And that truth is that you did everything that you could. There wasn't one more thing you could've done. Can you live in that moment, as best you can, with clear eyes, and love in your heart? With joy in your heart? If you can do that, gentlemen, then you're perfect![13]

That's who my parents were. That's who I want to be, and who I sometimes am. It reminds me in a weird way of a math equation that most people have a hard time accepting 1=.999... My first thought reading that was, "Well, that's obviously wrong." But it's not, and there are proofs. The simplest one is arrived at by writing out this equation as a fraction:
.333...=1/3rd
1/3rd x 3=1
therefore .333... x 3 also=1

This is still not convincing to some people, but there are more rigorous proofs that you can look up on some mathematics pages, or you can ask a serious mathematician yourself. They all agree. The beautiful message I get out of this formula is that if you are forever getting infinitely closer to 1, then you are 1. I never expected math to sound so wonderfully Buddhist to me, but there it is. And it makes me think of my parents, and fortitude, and the wonderful realization that no matter what the circumstances of your life may be, no matter what is happening, no matter how you are feeling, if you are trying your best, and you refuse to give up, refuse to stop, then you're perfect. Maybe not all the time, and that's OK, but sometimes, you can be perfect if you persevere, if you have fortitude.

If you are suffering from depression or anxiety, you will probably need some help, because that makes everything harder. See a doctor; get some professional help. Things are rarely as hopeless as they seem, and we can usually do more than we think we can, but sometimes we need help to see that.

I haven't even mentioned dogs in this chapter, but it was through working with dogs that I developed the virtue of fortitude. I was terrified when I started working with dogs. My first dog-care jobs were in grooming and doggie daycare; I never felt like I knew what I was doing and my self-confidence, which was never great, was at an all-time low. I remember one day after I had given my notice that I was leaving the grooming job I had at the time, I was driving in for one of the last days and I was very upset. I felt like a failure, and this was after having already failed to find a job in politics (the field I studied in college, and my last job before moving to Toronto). I was crying on my way to work, and I just felt like giving up.

I started working with dogs to help me deal with the pain of losing Kayla, my beloved 19-year-old cocker spaniel, and I started feeling like I failed her too. I became angry, and I don't know who or what I was angry with, but I'm fairly sure it was mostly at the idea of failure itself, as a concept, or idea, and not at any person, not even myself. I found myself *literally* screaming, angrily and at the top of my lungs, "I WILL NEVER GIVE UP! NEVER!!" And I meant it. I started to calm down a little bit and think about what I needed to do next. I decided I needed to learn more about dog behavior, and not just enough to be a better groomer; I wanted to be a dog trainer. I wanted to destroy that feeling that I had failed Kayla and destroy it I did. I did not fail her. I struggled, I nearly failed, but I kept trying. I didn't give up.

At that moment, I was Jean and Joe Josselyn's son. I had fortitude. I was perfect.

Prudence

Prudence, or "seeing ahead": a disciplined approach to planning ahead.

"Dear Prudence" is one of my favorite Beatles songs. I've always thought it was about the value of loosening up and having fun, because they repeatedly invite Prudence to play with them. The Beatles are practically begging Prudence to come out and have some fun in this song. The virtue of prudence, for me, is about setting realistic goals and methodically working towards them, so that you can enjoy the fruits of your labor in fun, spontaneous ways.

The first dog-training class I took was called "Foundation Skills." It was a modern, science-based class and they were very thorough in teaching us the basics of classical and operant conditioning and how we can use this knowledge to better train our dogs. The purpose was to give us a firm foundation, hence the name, so that we would have the tools needed to work our way through the challenges that we would inevitably face. This foundation is what makes it possible for me to write well-thought-out, methodical training plans for clients to follow, based on what we worked on in our sessions. The training plan is crucial, because we need to plan ahead, to set goals, and to follow through, and a training plan gives us a clear way to do that.

We need to exercise prudence, which is defined as: "the quality or fact of being prudent, or wise in practical affairs, as by providing for the future."[14] Modern dog training has taught me the value of planning ahead and starting off with a firm foundation and building on it in a methodical manner. That may not sound like fun, but it *is*. It's fun because it works, and having some success at something that is important to you is thrilling.

Prudence is also sometimes seen as synonymous with caution. It's good to be cautious, provided we aren't letting ourselves get too fearful. "Dear Prudence" was written about a real person, Prudence Farrow, but I think they're also trying to say something more generally about the value of loosening up and having fun, and not being overly cautious, or *too* prudent. I think that's what the Beatles were trying to say with the chorus in that song. I would have *Loved* to have had a conversation about the virtue of prudence with John Lennon, or anything really, since I'm a lifelong Beatles fan.

I doubt the Beatles were arguing that prudence itself is a bad thing to be shunned in favor of playing and having fun, but I do suspect that many other people see prudence primarily as boring and prefer being spontaneous and having fun. There is no conflict between planning ahead and being spontaneous and having fun. Prudent planning can give you the moments of freedom and the confidence you need to have spontaneous fun.

My favorite example of prudent planning leading to spontaneous fun came from a dog-training workshop I took in New York that was part of my dog-trainer training. The class recruited people from the neighborhood who had never had any formal training, and we had to teach them to walk their dog on a loose leash with no pulling from one end of the classroom to the other, and the room was *looooong*! My students were a petite woman and a massive dog that looked to be part Newfie, part Great Dane, and part ... buffalo? (He was YUUUUGE!) ... who was usually walked with a prong collar. This was my *very first* attempt to train any dog owner to teach their dog how to do anything, and I was nervous. Steve, the instructor, did a great job getting us ready for this. He explained how we teach the dog to follow us on a loose leash, what to do if the dog starts to pull, and made sure we had practiced our timing and mechanical skills in advance as well. He was very prudent, and because I carefully and prudently followed his trustworthy advice, I had *so much fun!*

   As soon as the class was over, he asked who wanted to describe how things went and my hand spontaneously shot in the air as I exclaimed, "ME FIRST, ME FIRST! OH MY GOD THAT WAS SO MUCH FUN! I WAS SO NERVOUS BUT IT WAS SO MUCH FUN!" I wasn't usually the first person to speak up in that class; this was a spontaneous, out-of-character reaction, and I didn't even wait for him to call on me. As soon as he looked in my direction, I was blurting out how much fun I had had. He laughed and said, "Good! Dog training is supposed to be fun! If it's not, you're probably doing something wrong!"

   I do feel the need to point out "fun" doesn't always mean "easy." There is some work we must put in to get the fun, spontaneous results we Love to share with our dogs. Having fun with our work makes it easier, but it is still work. Buffy and Spike, like nearly all dogs, Love to shove their face into the dirt and grass during walks. I Love to let them do that because it makes them happy, but they often get a little grass and some twigs in their hair, which can be both unsightly and uncomfortable. Spike will let me do anything grooming-related because I took things as slowly as he needed me to, but he can get impatient if it goes on for a long time, or if I am working on Buffy instead. So, I keep the trimming sessions short and take turns. I trim some of Spike's hair, treat and praise him, then I do some of Buffy's hair, treat and praise her, and go back and forth that way for a while until either they've had enough, or we're done. Now with their chins neatly trimmed, they can bury their face into an interesting scent and not have a lot of debris stuck in their hair, so we immediately go for a nice long walk. Buffy and Spike get to bury their faces into all sorts of nice smells that they really Love. I get to watch them have loads of fun without having to dig a lot of junk out of their hair. Buffy, Spike, and I are able to enjoy spontaneous, exuberant fun, because I took the time to teach them to be comfortable getting beard trims, with prudent planning.

Steve used to tell us to have a fun, stress-free play session with our dogs after training. This was to help the dog learn that while our training sessions require some thoughtful effort on the part of the dog, those efforts will be rewarded, and will be followed by some fun play, as fun and spontaneous as you want it to be. *We* need to learn that lesson as well. Prudent planning ahead is not boring if we're doing it right. If we plan ahead and don't cut corners, we will find that our results are more than just satisfying, more than merely practical: We will discover that a little prudence carefully applied can give us results that are thrilling, results that make it possible for us and our dogs to fully enjoy and embrace our fun-Loving, spontaneous, playful side.

Today, before doing some training with my dog, I was singing Dear Prudence to myself. Buffy and Spike looked at me curiously, as they often do, and after carefully putting on their leashes and collars, grabbing some of their favorite treats and toys, our clicker for some clicker training, I walked over to the door. Buffy and Spike were waiting patiently because they knew I was getting ready to take them out, and that causing a big fuss would just slow the process down. They were exercising a little prudence of their own, so I invited them to join me outside to go for a walk and to have some fun playtime- **And then we did!**

Temperance

Temperance: humility, self-restraint, moderating the desires, not just seeking one's own pleasure.

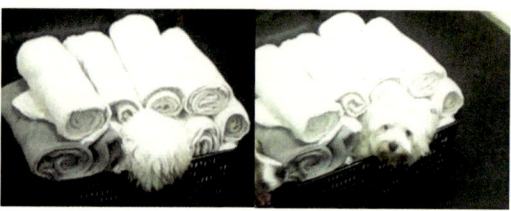

I learned a lesson in humility while writing this chapter. When I went back to re-read it, it became clear to me that it was not good. I might even go so far as to say it sucked. I was pleased that some of the problems I identified were the same as some of the problems my husband identified, because it meant that I could recognize some of the flaws in my own work. One of my heroes, hardcore wrestling icon Mick Foley, made that observation about a screenplay he tried to write after having already written a bestselling autobiography. When he read the screenplay over in typescript, he decided that it wasn't good. He mentioned this to a friend who was also a writer, and his friend surprised him by saying that he had a gift most writers would never have: the ability to be objective about his own work.[15] Being able to fairly and objectively evaluate your own work is, as Mick Foley realized, a gift. I Love gifts, but at the moment what I *really* wanted was a chapter on temperance, and I didn't have one. I still *didn't know* what I *did* want to write. I stared blankly at the screen for a long time saying, "*I don't know,*" and that's when I had a breakthrough: I have learned to be humble enough to comfortably say "*I don't know*" in recent years.

Many years ago on social media, I had another lesson in humility. I had an argument online with an academic (a friend of a friend), whose degree was in economics, about one of the central claims in a popular book called *Freakonomics* by economist Steven D. Levitt and journalist Stephen J. Dubner (2005). The claim was that the reason crime rates dropped throughout the 1990s and 2000s was because abortion had been legalized over a generation before. They had a lot of statistics from many different countries to back it up, and I believed them. The argument seemed very convincing to me. I was just dead wrong, and he decisively proved me wrong with multiple studies and journal articles. The *Freakonomics* authors made a simple math error and other serious economists spotted it easily, but apparently his publisher did not. It's still an extremely entertaining book that expanded my understanding of how broad a topic economics can be, but on this particular point it was wrong.

I'm not a serious economist, but I've taken several economics classes and thought I was reasonably well informed. By the end of the discussion, it was painfully clear I was completely out of my league. Being wrong often feels unpleasant, but after a couple days of arguing, I couldn't get around the fact that I was wrong, and he was right. He was a serious pro, he knew his stuff, and he could prove it multiple ways. My first instinct was to look for a way to save face or cast doubt on what he was saying. Instead, the last thing I typed was, "Well, that looks pretty conclusive to me. Thanks for sharing the links and your patience." I was gritting my teeth as I typed it, but I felt relieved after I posted the last response. I admitted an uncomfortable truth and felt good about myself after I did it.

This was years ago, and looking back on it now, I think it might have been the most useful argument I've ever had. I learned something new, it appropriately humbled me, and I didn't let my ego ruin it for me. I feel pride when I look back on it now. I don't always handle arguments that well. I probably need a few more experiences like that. I think we all do. I hope someone politely, patiently, and appropriately humbles you, and that you grow enough as a person to thank them for it.

We're all flawed, we're all mortal, and none of us knows everything. Being confronted with something we don't know can be frustrating, but it's a normal part of life that we all share, and it can be an opportunity for learning.

Several years ago, I was confronted with the reality that I did not know as much about dogs as I thought I did. This was a difficult, uncomfortable realization, but it inspired me to learn more about modern dog training and behavior, and learning is a beautiful thing. Sometimes the thing we need to learn is, "I don't have enough information to know this," or "This is not a high priority; I can better spend my time learning or doing other things." You don't need to have an answer to every question; there's no need to form an opinion on every topic. It is inevitable that you will find yourself in situations in which the only really truthful thing you can say is, "I don't know." We often don't want to admit that when we're working with our dogs, so we make up reasons to explain the things we don't know. Sometimes we anthropomorphize and apply human expectations. I've had many clients say their dog Loves to relax and peacefully enjoy the scenery in the back yard. Then a squirrel enters the yard and the dog goes absolutely ballistic. That dog was not peacefully enjoying the scenery; he was on guard duty, as indicated by a stiff body posture and intense stares out the window. Sometimes we make up standards that don't really apply, like when we see a dog pulling on leash and say, "She's being dominant." How do we know she doesn't just need to pee *really bad* and wants to get to her favorite potty area?

Modern dog training spends a lot of time trying to understand our dog's emotional state, studying body language, tone, energy level, panting levels, etc., in response to different situations, but we spend at least as much time, maybe even more, studying behavior, because behavior is easier to measure. Our dog's emotional state is obviously *extremely important*, but even the best dog trainers will sometimes misinterpret a dog's emotional state. Behavior is much easier to observe and measure. Working with dogs has made me a lot more *comfortable* recognizing the fact that while measuring behavior can give us some insights into our dog's emotional state, because behavior is driven by our thoughts and feelings, we don't really know for sure what is going on in the heads and hearts of our dogs, or even other people. That comfortable recognition makes it much easier to be humble. Humility is the foundation of temperance.

When I first started working with dogs, I was trained by people who believed in the outdated and discredited alpha male model of dog training. Watching reality-TV dog-training shows had given me the same misinformation as millions of other dog Lovers, so I was receptive. I became emotionally attached to that model because it was explained to me by people I trusted, and I believed that it was what I needed to do in order to work with dogs, which I very much wanted to do. I even had arguments with people online defending these outdated notions. Some of the people I was arguing with were clearly not only more experienced and knowledgeable than me; they were actual scientists and researchers who were more experienced and knowledgeable *than the people I learned from.* Acknowledging I was on the wrong path was unpleasant because, as I said, I had become emotionally attached to these discredited ideas. It is not easy to admit you don't know something, especially if you thought you did. We need to learn to be humble enough to admit the fact that some of our most cherished beliefs are just wrong, and that's not easy. Some of our beliefs are formed in groups we want to remain a part of, and we get emotionally attached to the group and the beliefs that are shared.

The attachment to our groupthink beliefs can last

even after we've rejected those beliefs and left the group where those beliefs were formed. When I went through my foundational dog-training course with the Karen Pryor Academy, I had already made up my mind to pursue modern, positive reinforcement training, as had every other student in that class. During one of our assessments, one of my fellow students, Bob, was having a very hard time with his dog Sparky. He was trying to get him through some agility obstacles and the dog was getting it wrong over 50% of the time. Bob was visibly frustrated the whole time and was reprimanding the dog verbally in a frustrated manner. He knew (as we all did) that this was not the best way to handle Sparky's distracted state. Steve, our instructor, took Bob aside and gently reminded him that Sparky was being affected by Bob's reprimands, and they were both becoming more distressed. I didn't hear the conversation but based on similar situations I have found myself in, I am pretty sure it went something like:

"Sparky isn't being stubborn, he's a good dog and you're a good trainer. Sparky will probably do better tomorrow. If not, maybe he's not feeling well, and we should have him checked out. You may not know why Sparky isn't performing right now, and that's OK, but the reprimands are *clearly not helping. Trust* what you've learned and the work you've put in." Bob and Sparky nailed it the next day, almost perfectly. Bob exercised a little self-restraint, didn't let himself get frustrated, and was more patient. Sparky was happy to perform now that Bob was no longer getting frustrated with him. It seemed likely that at least part of the problem on the previous day were all the reprimands and Bob's tone.

I think what Steve said to Bob may, in some sense, have been similar to what some people refer to as "tone policing," but was very different in important ways: Steve was *not* complaining about the way Bob was dealing with him or with Sparky, he was pointing out that maybe Sparky was being affected by Bob's tone. Dogs have a *lot* less power than we do, and as I noted earlier, with greater power comes greater responsibility. Steve didn't scold Bob or judge him; he just got Bob to listen to Sparky. If there was any tone policing going on, it was Bob appropriately and successfully tone policing himself. That is something I think we should all strive to do more, because I don't think any of us do it as often as we should.

The way we speak to dogs, and other people, affects them. Our tone, the things we say, and the *way* we say them matters. Since your dog can't ever really master English or any other human language, they rely on things like facial expressions, body language, and *tone* more than we do. Your dog may be even better at reading body language than you are. If you become angry with him, he will know, and it will hurt him. If you become angry with any animal that can read your tone, like dogs and humans, you may hurt them. The old saying, "Sticks and stones may break my bones, but words will never hurt me," is a well-meaning fiction. Angry words spoken with an unpleasant tone hurt every bit as much as being slapped in the face, sometimes more. Emotional pain activates the same part of the brain that physical pain does, and it's just as real.

Tone policing has a much-deserved bad reputation because it's often used by powerful people to dismiss or divert attention away from the complaints of less powerful people. When working with dogs, I will tolerate a *lot* of angry displays without returning that anger, because the power gap between us is enormous. I won't ignore the anger and pretend it doesn't matter. I'll try to understand the cause and I will try to change the dog's emotional state. I'll give her chances to learn a different reaction and reward her if she responds appropriately. I will try my best to help. But I will not express any anger towards her, even if inside I am starting to feel angry. I will instead exercise some self-restraint, check my anger and my tone, and try my best to help her cope with whatever has upset her so she can respond happily in the future. I don't resent her anger because I know that I have all the control in the relationship, and I also know the causes of her anger are probably valid and complex. She may or may not have good reasons for hating me personally, but she almost certainly has some very good reasons for being upset, even if we don't know what they are. If that dog never stops hating me, I'm still probably going to be just fine. But if I started to hate that dog, I might not be willing to work with him at all, or even offer a referral to another trainer. If I fail to help an angry dog in a training session because I am just as angry with him as he is with me, that dog may not get the help it needs; it might get surrendered, or even euthanized. There are times when I have life and death power over a dog. If I let anger inform any of my actions in those scenarios, I could end up ruining, or even ending, the life of a dog that is essentially powerless and needs my help. That would damage me in ways it scares me even to contemplate, and it would be much worse for the dog. I need to be able to exercise self-restraint to do my job.

I do feel strongly that everyone should be treated with dignity and respect, and we should all try to be civil to each other, but it's not always easy. I have always Loved and admired the Loving, forgiving, peaceful way that Martin Luther King and Gandhi always conducted themselves. They never hated their oppressors, and even preached Love and forgiveness for them. Most of us aren't Martin Luther King or Gandhi. Loving an oppressor the way King and Gandhi did is awe inspiring and a noble goal, but it's not easy, and I don't think it's fair to hold any oppressed or marginalized person to such a standard. We can and should express admiration for someone who is able to exercise self-restraint even when dealing with oppressors, but criticizing someone who is angry because they've been treated badly is unfair. Even Gandhi and King were angered by oppression, as we should all be. It may be better to forgive and Love oppressors the way King and Gandhi did, but I can't blame an oppressed person for being angry with their oppression and their oppressors. That's a natural and often involuntary reaction.

It's much easier for powerful people to be gracious and understanding when faced with unpleasant treatment, and we should hold them to that. I quoted Stan Lee (writing as Spider-Man's Uncle Ben) earlier noting that, "with great power comes great responsibility." Those with more power have more responsibility. We should insist on civility from our political leaders and other powerful people, in the same way, and for the same reason that modern dog trainers (and dogs like Sparky!) insist that all dog caregivers treat dogs with civility. Powerful people that punch down angrily at those less powerful should not be allowed to exercise power. Dog trainers that cannot keep their anger in check should not be dog trainers. Political leaders that are incapable of keeping their anger in check should not be political leaders.

We can and should tone police *ourselves, especially* when dealing with those that have less power than we do. But if someone (dog or human) is becoming angry with us, instead of tone policing them, we need to ask ourselves honestly and humbly if they've got a legitimate grievance. Power relationships vary wildly between people, but we're all far more powerful than our dogs, and we have a lot more responsibility to monitor our tone. People often angrily reprimand a dog for growling, even though their own tone is usually a lot more unpleasant than the mild growl the dog gave. Growling is just information; it's not an attack and should never be reprimanded. Instead exercise a little humility and self-restraint, be as civil as possible, and try to figure out how you can make things better, because that's what we all want in our relationships with our dogs and each other. As one of my hubby's heroes, Miss Manners, once said:

> The whole country wants civility. Why don't we have it? It doesn't cost anything. No federal funding, no legislation is involved. One answer is the unwillingness to restrain oneself. Everybody wants other people to be polite to them, but they want the freedom of not having to be polite to others. Unfortunately, it doesn't work that way.[16]

Most of us accept that it's important for dogs to learn self-restraint and moderate their desires (don't jump up, don't bark, don't pull on leash), but it's also important for us to moderate our desires. and not just for obvious things like sex and drugs, which is what I usually think of first when someone says, "moderate the desires." Moderating those desires *is* necessary, because they can turn into unhealthy obsessions. But it also means tempering your desire to be right and proving the other *wrong*: to "win." Competitiveness has its benefits; I think of myself as a very competitive person, and I Love winning. But not everything is a fight; *most* things aren't a fight. A training session should never be a confrontation, nor should a discussion or debate. Unfortunately, they often are.

The way we speak to each other is often less polite than it should be, especially when it comes to things like politics and religion. The way we talk to each other isn't the only major problem though; our goals and our actions are also often not honorable. We have a very strong desire to "win" arguments. Often when an online argument ends with one person leaving the discussion, the person remaining boasts that they "won." What did they win? I've never seen an "I just embarrassed a troll" trophy and I don't think anyone's giving out cash prizes either. "Winning" an online argument may be the most useless thing a person can do with their time. I would know; I've wasted a *ton*. Sadly, we aren't usually interested in *learning* anything in these arguments. I once saw an interview with Jordan Peterson in which he was asked about his opposition to legislation banning discrimination and after some tough (but fair!) questioning from comedian Jim Jefferies, he admitted he was wrong about the Civil Rights Act and acknowledged it did make things better. Every article I saw on this interview stated "Peterson *destroyed* by Jim Jefferies" or something similar. I am not a Jordan Peterson fan. I've never read his books and I don't know much about him. What little I do know I am uncomfortable with. But he was not in any way "destroyed" here. He was presented with an argument he couldn't respond to, and honestly admitted he was wrong. That isn't destruction, that's personal growth. That's a good thing that we should desire far more than "winning" any fight over politics, or dog training methods.

Unfortunately, reality TV shows have taught us that winning in these contexts is often defined as making the other give up. A dog licks his lips and turns his head to the side and down, with ears pinned back, and you think you "won" because the dog is now "calm/submissive." A person you argued with on social media left the discussion thread, or maybe even blocked you, and you think you "won." You win nothing by making the other submit. You have not learned anything new; you have not grown; you don't get a trophy. You won nothing at all.

We all need to remember that *our* beliefs and desires, whether they be physical, social, or political, are not the only ones that matter. One of the best ways to learn this is to take your dog for a walk. You may have a desire to get some exercise and peacefully enjoy the fresh air. Your dog may have a desire to check their pee-mail and sniff everything, and run up to every dog and say hi, pulling you off your feet. You could use corrections and reprimands to force your dog to comply with your demands, and because of the power gap between you that will probably work. But then your dog's desires are being completely ignored, and your dog may let you know in unpredictable and unpleasant ways. They may become leash reactive and aggressive, or depressed and shut down, refusing to walk. If, however you moderate your own desires, and teach the dog to moderate their desires, you can both win. Teach the dog that *not* pulling and choosing to walk by your side instead means they *can* sniff this bush and that fire hydrant and say hi to that nice golden retriever next door. By moderating our own desire to control the walk by force and instead teaching the dog to follow us, we get to have our desire for a peaceful, relaxing walk met. The dog gets their desire to sniff things and say hi met by moderating those desires so that they can resist the impulse to pull.

One of the miraculous things about modern dog training is that we learn to consider their desires as well as our own. When we do that, we can treat them with the same dignity and respect with which we would like to be treated. We need to care about the wellbeing and happiness of others, because if you're the only one who's happy, you won't be happy for long. We're social animals; the happiness of others *will* affect us. This is what makes the Golden Rule practical. If we all follow it, it will benefit all of us, and there *is no limit* to what we can eventually accomplish over time. But it's hard. We naturally see things from our own perspective, we have more control over our lives than over anyone else's, so our life is going to be our first responsibility. But we need to remember everyone has the same limited perspective, personal biases and individual responsibilities that we do.

Humility, self-restraint, moderating the desires, and genuinely caring about the happiness of others, and *not* just our own, is what constitutes temperance. It takes some humility to admit the desires of others are as valid as our own, and some self-restraint to treat others as we would like to be treated. But virtuous living requires it, and we need to cultivate the virtue of temperance in ourselves if we are to follow the Golden Rule. Cultivating temperance, along with trust, hope, Love, prudence, justice, and fortitude, together, is what makes following the Golden Rule possible. If we *all* work on cultivating these virtues and following the Golden Rule, eventually, *anything will be possible.*

ANYTHING.

The Beam in My Eye

Why do you notice the splinter in your neighbor's eye, and not the beam in your own eye? Remove the beam from your own eye first, and then you will be able to see more clearly and remove the splinter from your neighbor's eye.

—Matthew 7:3-5

I Love working with people and their dogs, but there are times when it can be a little heartbreaking. I often work with reactive, aggressive dogs who require a lot of work and patience, and Loving parents who need some support and understanding. Most of them can be helped with time, patience, and a little effort. People who take on a hard job like that have my respect and admiration, because they're saving lives. One of the saddest things I ever hear is when one of these heroic dog adopters gets scolded by another dog owner while they're out on a walk: "You really should get him trained." "You obviously can't handle that dog!" "It's not the dog's fault, it's your fault!" If you have ever said anything similar to or about another dog or dog owner, please stop. All these statements are unfair and cruel.

Here's a common scenario. You have your well-behaved dog trotting along by your side with no leash, because you took the time to train your dog to give you eye contact regularly, come when called every time, and to stick close to you on walks. You get around the corner, minding your own business, when suddenly another dog starts barking and lunging at you and your dog. As the embarrassed owner pulls their dog away, you pick up your startled, perfectly innocent dog, and yell at the other person to be more careful with their dog. The uncomfortable truth here is that in this scenario *you* are the one engaging in bad behavior. There are thousands of reactive dogs across the city, dogs that *must,* for their own safety and that of others, stay on leash whenever they are outside. When a fearful dog that is on leash is suddenly confronted with an energetic dog that is *off l*each, their fear response often explodes. This is because they *know* the other dog can do whatever they want, while they are trapped, attached to a leash they cannot get away from. This is why we have leash laws. If you are walking around with an off-leash dog, you need to be 100% certain that you will *not* cross the path of any fearful or aggressive dog. If you allow this to happen, the first thing you should do is apologize while you are gathering your dog up and leaving the scene. The next thing you should do is buy a leash and use it. Because while you may be judging the other person, there are going to be other people nearby that know better, and they will judge *you* and your behavior harshly. "Judge not, that you be not judged." (Matthew 7:1 RSV.)

I felt myself getting angry as I typed that last paragraph. I must remind myself not to be judgmental too. I have this beam in my eye, metaphorically speaking, making it hard to see things clearly. It's smaller than it used to be, but still a problem. It used to make me say things like, "Bad dog!" and, "She's stubborn," or "She's dominant." I almost never say things like that now, but I still find myself saying things like, "He's a horrible person," and, "What a jerk!" regularly, even though I don't really think any of us are smart enough, or good enough, or fair enough to make judgments like that about anyone. Ever.

You have a similar beam, or beams, in your eye. I know this because if you are reading this, you are human. Every single one of us is flawed, biased, and makes mistakes every single day. But we still have an unreasonably high degree of confidence in our views, even though we can look at the world around us and see countless examples of people just like us getting things wrong. It's unreasonable to think we aren't also getting things wrong. Many of us recognize that it's poor behavior when others judge a reactive dog or their Loving adopter for aggressive outbursts by the dog. I don't think most of us recognize that judging the judgmental person is also poor behavior.

One of my first clients had several rescue dogs she needed help with. The last one she adopted was a 12-year-old chihuahua named Fez who was recovering from a badly broken jaw after a lifetime of physical abuse. This poor dog was absolutely terrified of every person and every dog he met. But my friend Rebecca just wanted to make sure the last few years of his life were better than the first twelve. She doesn't think of herself as a hero, and that makes her even more of a hero to me. She put in a lot of work with that dog, and when I saw her again a couple years later to start doing canine nosework with another one of her dogs, I saw Fez again. He was still alive, he remembered me, and he was happy to see me. *He was happy to see me!!* His tail was wagging, his body language was loose and wiggly, and he was soliciting affection! He wanted me to pet him, and he rubbed against my leg gratefully when I did. He also had dementia and would sometimes snap because he got very confused, but he didn't do any harm and he recovered quickly. To that dog, what Rebecca did for him was the greatest miracle possible in his little life, and I am just glad I was able to see it and be some small part of the process. This was still early days in my dog-training career, and I was making very little money, but no amount of money would have been as rewarding as seeing a totally innocent animal, who had probably never known real happiness before, finally experience the happy, fulfilling life he always deserved. There's nothing better than that. Nothing.

Some of the nicest clients I've had, like Rebecca, have been people who adopted an older, fearful, abused dog like Fez and saved its life by giving it a Loving home. More than once, these heroic clients have told me that they've been publicly shamed by other dog owners. That infuriates me, but I have to remind myself not to make the mistake of judging or shaming them in the same way. That's why I chose the example of the off-leash dog and owner approaching the reactive dog and owner: it highlights inappropriate, judgmental behavior not just by others, but also by me. I am quick to defend friends and clients who are being unfairly judged by people violating leash laws, and that will continue. But I don't need to shame or attack the person doing the judging. I don't know enough to judge them that harshly. Maybe they don't normally have their dog off leash, they were just in a hurry this one time; maybe they're usually more understanding; maybe they have mental health issues; maybe they just don't know any better. I can't look inside another person's (or dog's) head or heart and understand why they do the things they do. I don't even know if people have free will. Scientists and philosophers are still trying to figure that out and, without knowing that, I don't have enough information to judge their character fairly.

We tend to do a fairly good job *not* judging dogs. Even the people who cruelly judge other dog owners usually don't judge the dog; that's why they use the phrase, "It's not the dog, it's the *owner*." I'm glad they're not judging the dog; they don't know the dog's history, or what issues the dog may be struggling with, or how it was raised. I wish we also recognized that we don't know enough about other *people's* history—what issues they're dealing with related to physical or mental health, or how they were raised, or what they've had to endure—to judge them either. We don't really know how much of our behavior is related to nature or nurture; many scientists don't even think we have free will. I have no idea if they're right. My best guess is we *can* have free will, but it's a struggle, because we're constantly being pushed and pulled in many directions at once, many of us have mental health problems or cognitive disabilities, and we all sometimes find ourselves doing things we later wish we had not.

One of the few times we are fair and nonjudgmental is when someone dies. When a famous politician dies, we tend to rethink our judgment of them. Many progressive liberal Democrats who hated Antonin Scalia when he was alive heaped praise on him for his warm friendship with Ruth Bader Ginsburg, his great affection for many people he strongly disagreed with, and his obvious intelligence. They did *not* pretend to like everything he did; they judged his decisions just as negatively as they did before he died, but they stopped lying to themselves about their ability to judge his character. Many people who disliked both Presidents Bush wept openly when they saw George W. Bush eulogize his father George H. W. Bush, especially when W. called him, "The best father a son or daughter could ever ask for," and broke down himself. I never voted for either of them, but that moment hurt me. I had always disliked them both, and that moment reminded me of every unfair, judgmental thing I ever said about either of them. Some people will post hateful things at these moments like, "I'm not going to pretend that jerk is an angel just because he died!" That's heartbreaking. Death is something most of us don't like thinking about, and something we are all probably in denial about. It's also a tremendous source of suffering that we all share. When it comes to Death, we're all victims; we're all in danger. Most of us will watch death take our parents from us, and our pets, and we know death awaits us as well, and even though it may not happen until after we're gone, we know death is the fate that ultimately awaits our children. Death will take everyone and everything you ever Loved away from you. You are lying if you say you aren't frightened by that. Death unites us all.

There are some rare, extreme examples where we are so incredibly horrified by the evil a person did in their lifetime that we are relieved that they are dead, because that means they can't hurt anyone anymore. The most obvious example is Hitler. I am glad he died, and the world is a better place without Hitler on it. I would have been *far* gladder if he had repented of his evil plans before he carried them out, long before he died. I will not wish pain and suffering on anyone, not even Hitler. I will instead remind myself that even Hitler was once a newborn baby crying for his mother. I will never stop being horrified by what he did. I will never stop being glad he can't do any more harm. I can and do hate, with real passion, the evil he did. If I am going to be completely honest, I must admit that I do hate Hitler, but I don't think I should. I think I should remember that even Hitler was once a small baby that wanted to be Loved, and I *can* feel Love and pity for that baby. I can't maintain that attitude though. When I think about adult Adolf, I inevitably end up hating him again. But we don't have to, and we should try not to. Hatred has its place. Hatred can sometimes have its uses. We should hate cruelty, oppression, injustice, and death, but never people or animals, no matter how much we hate what they did. That's awfully hard, and I'm not there yet, but I'm trying.

I'm a dog Lover, so I am incredibly happy that we're usually honest enough and humble enough to recognize that *none* of us can fairly judge the dogs we encounter in our lives. We can judge whether their behavior is desirable or not, but we can't definitively label them a

85

"bad" or "dominant" dog. There is too much about them, their history, their cognitive abilities, and their DNA, that we just don't know. My hope is that we all learn to refrain from judging each other in the same way that many of us have learned to stop judging our dogs. Whenever anyone judges the character of another person or dog, they're engaging in behavior that should be judged negatively. But that doesn't mean we can judge *them* and conclude that they're bad people. I am not qualified to make that judgment. I've still got this beam in my eye.

Virtuous Animals?

The question is not, Can they reason? nor, Can they talk? but, Can they suffer?

—Jeremy Bentham, *An Introduction to the Principles of Morals and Legislation*

Can animals be virtuous? Do they have any sense of morality? Do they merit moral considerability? Many scientists, going back to the Enlightenment, have believed the answers to each of those questions was no. This is changing, however, and has been for years. Very few scientists today would argue animals merit no moral considerability. As Bentham righty observed centuries ago, animals can suffer, they are aware of their suffering, and if we are to consider ourselves moral beings, the suffering of others *must* matter to us. Animals deserve moral considerability. That question, at least, is settled amongst most reasonable people.

But can animals *be* moral or virtuous? That's a harder question, but I am strongly inclined to answer yes. Science has shown that fewer than 0.5% of dog play-fights turn into actual conflict.[17] My work in doggie daycare for many years appears to confirm this, at least when I am working in a modern, professional day care. When you see dogs negotiating play, you can see them assessing their playmates' reactions, sometimes tentatively, adjusting, and expressing happiness or irritation with the responses they get. Many will "ask" before engaging in play and will break off play if the other gets upset. Not always, though. I have seen real fights break out. Lots of dogs can be a little too pushy for their playmates, just like people. I have always thought that dogs really do know that they have thoughts, feelings, and desires, and realize other dogs and other animals (like people) do as well, and that this matters to them. It does seem to me that on a rudimentary, basic level, dogs and many other animals have something that scientists refer to as a "theory of mind." Theory of mind is the understanding that others have thoughts, beliefs, feelings, and perspectives that are different from one's own. This is controversial and scientists disagree with each other. I don't expect this to be resolved any time soon.

I've spent several years working in doggie daycare, watching dogs play, argue, relax, and nap together. I learned nearly as much about dogs just watching them co-exist together as I did in any one of the courses I've taken. There is one particular example of an interaction between two dogs that was, in my eyes, incredibly kind, caring, and virtuous. There was a small, anxious little dog named Lola that was tentatively trying to play with other dogs, but she was a little shy and nervous. There was another bigger dog that was constantly trying to bully her. I think he just wanted to play, but Lola was afraid, so we kept them separate. I was working with another experienced doggie daycare person, and we did a good job keeping them separate, until late in the afternoon when we messed up one time. The two dogs got a little too close to each other and just before I split them up, the bigger dog muzzle-punched Lola. I don't think it was aggressive, and it wasn't hard, but the little dog became terrified and hid in the corner. I felt awful. I tried to comfort the little dog and did not mess up again, but the poor little dog was scared and shaking in the corner and didn't trust me. I didn't blame her. I let her down and felt a little ashamed of myself. It's usually a lot of fun working with dogs, but it can often be heartbreaking. Most people who work with dogs do so because they Love them, so when something goes wrong, the feelings of guilt can be hard to bear.

A large Leonberger named Rosie slowly started to approach Lola after Lola let out a sad-sounding little whimper. It was that sad little sound that got Rosie's attention. I had done some work with Rosie, so I knew she was great with little dogs: gentle and affectionate. The little dog still seemed scared, but less scared of Rosie than me. Rosie approached Lola with her tummy on the ground, crawling towards her. Lola was still visibly anxious, but less so. She seemed a little curious. Rosie lay down on her side in front of little Lola, so her head was a little bit lower than Lola's. The tiny little dog looked down into Rosie's face as Rosie lay there motionless, and then Rosie started to paw at her gently, playfully, very slowly, and cautiously. Lola let Rosie touch her several times and she seemed to like this gentle giant that was so patiently trying to coax her into a friendly play session. Eventually she crawled on top of Rosie and they both had a fun, mutually enjoyable play session that ended with them taking a nap side by side. There were a lot of other dogs, and Rosie had fun playing with practically all of them. But she singled out the sad little anxious dog for special attention, ignoring all the other dogs and people. I can't know for certain, but it seemed clear to me at the time that Rosie wanted to help cheer up another dog that needed some cheering up. Rosie earned the trust of a dog that was losing hope by showing her a little Love. *That's my job*, and on that day, Rosie did it better than I did. She was more than a "good dog," she was virtuous. Dogs do not understand concepts like virtue and morality the way we do, and we can't hold them to the same standards, but they do appear to have at least some capacity for intentional, virtuous, moral behavior. In at least this one case, Rosie was every bit as virtuous as I was, maybe more so. If the exact same scene I just described had played out between children in a playground, we would all agree that human Rosie was acting in a kind, morally good, virtuous manner. I can't think of any reason why we shouldn't say the exact same thing about Leonberger Rosie.

This does not mean they are the same as us, of course. We are clearly more powerful than any other animal, by far. Our ability to change the world around us, to learn new things and pass that knowledge on, is one that only humans have truly mastered. There is some evidence that other animals can learn from each other, and pass that learning on to other animals in their family or pack, but not to the extent that we can. Some scientists try to use this argument to prove animals are inherently inferior to us, do not have any moral status, and cannot be virtuous. Certainly, it's true that animals are not as intelligent as we are, and they can't use language as we do. But if you look to our past at all the things that scientists *used to* believe about the differences between people and animals, you can see that one by one they keep getting eliminated.

The mathematician and philosopher René Descartes described animals as "machines,"[18] which has led some to believe that he thought animals were not sentient at all. There may be some scientists who still believe this, but nowhere near as many. When the EU's Treaty of Lisbon came into force in 2009, it amended the Treaty on the Functioning of the European Union (TFEU) Article 13 Title 2 to include the text "Since animals are sentient beings..."[19]

According to The Nonhuman Rights Project (NhRP), the following is a list of abilities that at one time or another were considered unique to humans. All of the things mentioned on this list have been observed in chimpanzees: episodic memory, self-consciousness, self-knowing, self-agency, referential and intentional communication, mental time-travel, numerosity, sequential learning, meditational learning, mental state modeling, visual perspective taking, understanding the experiences of others, intentional action, planning, imagination, empathy, metacognition, working memory, decision-making, imitation, deferred imitation, emulation, innovation, material, social, and symbolic culture, cross-modal perception, tool-use, tool-making, cause-and-effect. (Petition of NhRP v. Samuel Stanley.)[20]

Dr. Helene Guldberg has argued that the ability to pass information on to later generations and change the world around them is such a vastly overwhelming difference that it renders all other animals nonmoral, because only humans can be moral.[21] This cannot be correct. Our ability to make choices and teach others is a difference in degree, not in kind. Other animals can make choices and they can make their choices known to others, and to teach them; they just can't do it as well as we can. They have not and may not be able to really master it. But the difference being highlighted here is not a moral difference, but a difference of power. We are more powerful than any other animal, and it's not close. But power can be used for good or evil; it is not moral.

While it does usually seem to be the case, and we generally agree, that our dogs' decisions are often based more on biology and conditioning than actual "choice," how is that different from us? Your choices are going to be obviously impacted by an incomprehensible number of factors depending on where you live, your DNA, and your upbringing. Some scientists have now discovered that when we make choices, they can often trace the activity in our brain to a moment just *before* we made a choice, leading many to speculate that free will is an illusion. I don't believe that, but it does seem clear, at a minimum, that free will is not free. *If* it exists at all, it takes a lot of work to develop it.

This is not a question that is going to be cleared up

91

any time soon; philosophers and scientists have been debating this for centuries and we appear no closer to a definitive conclusion. Most philosophical debates over free will revolve around whether it's compatible or incompatible with determinism—the belief that all events are determined by prior causes. But there are widespread disagreements about determinism as well: some define it differently; some reject it completely. The only thing I can say about free will with any degree of certainty is, "I don't know."

Immanuel Kant argued that since morality is real and imposes real obligations that we ought to follow, we must be free to follow them, because "ought implies can."[22] Kant also believed that while we all desire to be happy, happiness is only a good thing when you deserve to be happy because you are following the moral law. Therefore, the greatest good will be when everyone acts in conformity with the moral law, and everyone is completely happy because they deserve to be. The fact that no one can become morally perfect in a human lifetime but (according to Kant) we all *ought* to strive ever closer to moral perfection because it is the greatest good to which we are called also implies the immortality of the soul, since "ought implies can," and the only way you can get to the greatest good is if you exist longer than a human lifetime.[23] I find that argument appealing, and I hope it turns out to be true, but it's not completely convincing. Implied is not the same as proved.

While we may or may not have free will, it seems likely that we will be better off if we believe we do. Studies conducted by psychologist Roy Baumeister in 2009 seem to indicate that believing there is no such thing as free will leads to more undesirable behaviors, like cheating and refusing to help others.[24] Author and philosopher Stephen Cave argues for the development of an FQ (freedom quotient) similar to IQ (intelligence quotient) to measure the extent to which we have abilities people tend to associate with free will: the ability to create choices, and to discern between those choices, and the will to stick with them.[25] The ability to defer gratification is one measurable ability that can increase our FQ or freedom quotient. A chicken is able to resist a yummy treat for up to six seconds in return for a larger reward; chimpanzees can do this for up to two minutes. Most of us can do it even longer than that. Deferred gratification is the foundation of a common behavior we teach our dogs: "Leave it!" (also known as "Doggie Zen!" I Love that!). We teach the dog in training sessions that if they "leave" something when we ask them to, they will get a tasty treat, and then they will *also* get the thing they left alone right after. A Zen master might say, "To get the treat, you must leave the treat!" We teach it this way so that if a dog sees something dangerous, like a chicken bone, they will expect us to give them a treat, and then let them have the chicken bone as well if they leave the chicken bone alone when we ask them to. We *can't* let them have a chicken bone, so they will be disappointed unless we are able to distract them with bonus treats and loads of verbal praise. But if we train this behavior correctly and regularly, the dog will know that 99 times out of 100 when they defer gratification and leave things when asked, they will get everything they wanted. We will have taught our dogs the value of deferred gratification and helped them increase their FQ. Dr. Cave quotes a therapist commenting on an earlier article in the *Atlantic* in his discussion of FQ:

> My goal, as a therapist, is to give a person a greater sense of control of their lives, and to allow them to feel they're capable of making better decisions… [and] to create new experiences for the patient, experiences that will allow her/him to develop the skills to alter his/her behavior in the future.[26]

That is also my job as a dog trainer, and it's something we all can and should work on in our own lives. It's not always easy, especially if undesirable behaviors have a long history and have become a habit. Habits are extremely powerful things and probably control more of our behavior than our conscious mind does. There's a famous case of a patient named Eugene Pauly who lost the ability to create new memories, which is detailed in the book *The Power of Habit* by Charles Duhigg. Eugene would sometimes go for a walk and while he was out he would completely forget which house was his. Somehow, he always found his way home, even though he couldn't tell you how to get to his house, or even recognize it. It was because his wife had taken him for walks around that block and, even though he could not remember those walks, his brain had developed the habit of walking around the block and knew how to do it. He'd pass markers in the neighborhood that served as a cue for his walk home, and then he'd go that way and end up home.[27] It's the same cue-behavior-reward loop that we use in dog training all the time, and Duhigg describes several practical tips for harnessing the power of habits. Much like dog training, it's best to start with small steps and get yourself some easy wins, and to try and identify what the cues are that are triggering your habits, and what rewards you are seeking. That's more complicated than it sounds, and it's often difficult, but it definitely can be done. Reading *The Power of Habit* and applying those lessons can help you increase your own FQ (freedom quotient.)

We can't judge dogs morally because we don't know how free they were in choosing their actions, but just as importantly, we can't judge each other morally for the same reason. It's a lot more tempting to judge humans morally because there isn't as much of a power gap, but we are flawed and imperfect creatures with only imperfect control over our thoughts and actions at best. We have no choice but to judge some behaviors as unacceptable or undesirable, or even "bad" and refuse to tolerate them. But we must not ever judge any person or animal to be "bad" and refuse to tolerate them. Ever. We do not know enough about free will to know how responsible anyone is for anything, and without knowing how responsible we are for our actions, we cannot fairly judge anyone. We just don't know enough. That is a hard fact for a lot of people to accept, but it was true when Jesus said it 2000 years ago and it still is today. We are overly attached to our judgments of others, and it's hard not to be. There are political figures I am literally incapable of not judging, no matter how hard I try. That's a character flaw of mine that I need to work on, and that's OK because I like to work on my character flaws. And it's a good thing too, as I am unlikely to run out of character flaws to work on before I die!

Humans and other animals are more alike than they are different, and none of us is wise enough or virtuous enough to make moral judgements about the character of any animal. We can make judgements about behaviors, or as some people used to say, "Hate the sin and not the sinner!" An even better thing to say is that you should not hate sinners *or* their sins; you should hate your sins, because they're the only ones you can really do anything about. I'm not sure you need to "hate" your sins. If you, as a fallible person, spend too much time hating your sins, you're probably going to be a very unhappy person gripped with deep self-loathing. But you must be aware that you have character flaws, and you should be spending a lot more time working on your own flaws than worrying about everyone else's.

One of the scientists I read for this book is Mark Bekoff, Professor Emeritus of Ecology and Evolutionary Biology at the University of Colorado, Boulder. He also cofounded, with Jane Goodall, Ethologists for the Ethical Treatment of Animals and writes a science column about animal emotion for *Psychology Today*. He once received a note from an eighth grader who asked: "Do we really need more science to know animals have emotions and that they suffer?" and, "Will we really learn anything that tells us it's ok to treat them with less respect and compassion – don't we really know enough right now?" His answer was no, we will never learn anything that tells us it's OK to treat them with less respect and compassion, and this is part of his explanation: "If scientific studies of animal cognition and animal emotions stopped today, other animals should be just fine and also benefit from what we already know *if we truly use the information we already have*. Indeed, we are compelled to use what we know because each and every life matters, because each and every life is intrinsically valuable."[28] Amen.

Relationships and Animals

*You know, I think everybody longs to be loved, and
longs to know that he or she is lovable. And,
consequently, the greatest thing that we can do is to
help somebody know that they're loved and capable
of loving.*

—Fred Rogers: America's Favorite Neighbor (television
documentary), 2003

I want to talk about someone who Loves me. His
name is Brandon and I Love him too. He's had an awfully
hard, unfair life, but that's never stopped him from being a
Loving, affectionate, good boy. He's a cattle dog/mastiff
mix, a little over a year old who was apparently abandoned
as a puppy before ending up in a shelter run by Toronto
Animal Services (TAS). He lived on the streets as a puppy,
which is awful, and then in a shelter, which is also not
good, a short time in a foster home, then a short time in an
adopted home, then back in a shelter, all in his first year of
life. I did some work with him after he was adopted the
first time and he had a lot of problems to deal with, but he
was wonderful. He Loved his adopted parents and they
Loved having such a great companion, but he had a lot of
problems to overcome. His leash manners were not good,
he could be unpredictably fear-aggressive, he had some

resource-guarding issues, and he developed a severe case of separation anxiety. He's pretty smart though and responded well to training. The separation anxiety was a ton of work, but we got through it. We were also able to get his leash manners under control, dealt with his resource guarding, and made progress with his fear-aggression. It wasn't quite enough progress though. He could look and sound scary when he was reactive, scaring his family and their guests. He's not dangerous to people, even though his fear-based reactivity makes him look scary. His reactivity is fearful, and he puts on a loud, dramatic, visually intense display when he's triggered, but only because he wants the thing that has scared him to go away, *not* because he wants to do harm. He has had many opportunities to hurt someone who scared him and the worst he ever did was grab with his teeth, usually choosing to bark and lunge instead. There was one grab in a dog park to an inappropriately pushy stranger that drew a little blood, but it sounded to me like it was just a scratch which was intended to be nothing more than a grab. If a dog tries to grab your arm and you pull away your arm fearfully, an accidental scratch is likely to be the result. But that's it, just a single shallow scratch, the worst reaction he has ever had to a person, and it was a relatively minor incident caused by inappropriate human behavior.

Unfortunately, Brandon's triggers were unpredictable, and it took him a long time to settle down after he'd had a bad reaction. This was too much for his family and they reluctantly surrendered him. I had spent a lot of time working with him and I was extremely attached. I had felt confident things were going to work out, so it was heartbreaking when they didn't. I wanted to adopt him myself but he's not good living with other dogs, and I have a dog that can be fearful of bigger dogs, and he would probably be better off in a house or a larger apartment away from the noise of the city as well. I also ended up being the one who drove him to the shelter for the second time in his life, because no one else could. I made sure we had a lot of fun that day, visiting friends, hanging out at a farm, playing, and running. Then when I dropped him off at the shelter, and I heard him barking and whimpering sadly for me to come back, it crushed me. I promised myself I'd visit him every week, take him for a walk and a little play, and just sit with him in the kennel, and I did, every week, even though it was over an hour away. I wanted to help him get adopted and make him a little less lonely while he was stuck there. He was always thrilled to see me. He didn't blame me for his situation, and he still trusted me. He's still one of my best friends.

One of the things Brandon has been doing the last several visits to express his friendship is to give me a big enthusiastic hug when I arrive to visit and before I leave. Many people don't know this, but most dogs aren't very fond of hugging. I didn't remember Brandon being a big hugger when I met him the first few times, but he is now! He jumps up, grabs me, and really presses firmly into my clothes and my face. After a few weeks of this I had a realization: he's scent-rolling me when he hugs me. Scent-rolling is when a dog rolls his body into some distinctive smell that they find interesting. They roll in it so they can save the smell on their fur. Smell is their most powerful sense, so scents are extremely important to them. The enormous amount of time many dogs spend stopping and smelling things on a walk is frustrating for some people, but it does show you just how important scent is to a dog. Brandon has been saving my scent on his fur when I go visit him. I have no mixed feelings about the fact that Brandon Loves to save the smell of urine-stained bushes, dead animals, and me on his fur. Urine stains and dead animals are gross to me, but I know how intensely most dogs Love them, and I am genuinely honored that Brandon values my scent that much too, if not more. I know this sounds weird, and kind of is weird, but the fact that Brandon likes *my* scent as much as a dead squirrel, is one of the nicest compliments I've ever gotten. He Loves me, and he wants something to remember me by. I've got pictures and videos. Brandon just has my scent, but that's probably better than a thousand pictures to him.

At this point, it's getting hard to logically justify the amount of time I spend with Brandon. There are so many dogs and families I could be helping, potentially saving lives. But something has changed, something has been created, and it's something beautiful: a relationship. Brandon and I are friends. We've created a relationship together and it's a valuable thing that I am willing to work for, because I'm grateful for it, and I'm quite sure Brandon is too. Relationships expand us, they help us grow, they create new opportunities and potential, and we become deeply emotionally attached to them. We can recognize the logic and the truth behind the kind of universal Love taught by the world's great religions and moral philosophers, but it can be difficult (but not impossible) to truly Love someone you have no relationship with. Brandon and I have gotten to know each other, to like each other, and we *matter* to each other. At this point, if I left his life completely because I wanted to help more dogs, I would feel like I betrayed my friend, and he would wonder why the most reliable friend he's ever had abandoned him. That's not an option for me at this point. The relationship is too important to both of us, and it would damage me too much, as a person, in ways I don't think I could predict, to just end it. I doubt very seriously I would be as much help to other people or to other dogs if I had to live with the guilt of knowing I betrayed someone that shared Love with me. If I believed Brandon was unadoptable, that would change things, because I would know that I couldn't do anything to help him get adopted. I would still feel terrible heartbreak knowing he'll never find a good home. I have lived with the pain of knowing someone I Loved was suffering and, as much as I hate it, I know I can survive it. I don't know if I could handle the pain of knowing someone I Love is hurting *combined with* the guilt of feeling I didn't try my best to help. I know Brandon is an adoptable dog. I know he can find a good home. He's a friend who needs my help, so he's going to get it for the rest of his life if he needs me. This isn't just good for Brandon; it's good for me. The Love I get from him when I visit is intense, and it makes me a better, happier person, and he feels the exact same way. That's what makes life worth living. That's what relationships with others give us.

Relationships are important. They make us more than what we were. We can do practically anything when we're cooperating, and it's easier to cooperate with someone that you Love and have a relationship with than a stranger. But there is a danger. Some of our relationships mark us as members of a group. I play darts as a hobby, and the dart-playing community in Toronto is a group I am a member of and therefore have a relationship with. There are many groups I belong to and have relationships with: I'm a citizen of two countries, the USA and Canada, I was raised a Catholic, I am in a same-sex marriage and live in Toronto's "gay village," I'm a college graduate, and I've generally identified with one of the major political parties in my two countries all my life. For all the benefits of group membership, we must never forget the worst dangers of groupthink: the kind of viciousness that can lead millions of ordinary people to slaughter their neighbors in the name of ethnic cleansing or religion. We are more powerful when we are in groups, and great power requires great responsibility. We should be looking to expand our groups and develop more relationships with more people, not shrink into comfortable bubbles, and we should always look at people outside our groups as potential insiders and never enemies. We may not have the same attachment or level of responsibility towards people outside the groups and other relationships we're in, but we can still treat them all with dignity and respect, just as we would hope for that same dignity and respect from them. Relationships can create just as many divisions as connections, and we must be careful not to let that happen, otherwise we will, in our personal lives, slide into the same conflict and discord that has dragged political discourse in the US to its worst, most dangerous level in my lifetime.

The best way to combat the increased anger and hatred taking over our public discourse is to forge more relationships with more people, including animals, who are different from us. One of the things that I am most inspired by is the way we have learned to form relationships with other animals despite the fact that we do not share a common language or compatible DNA, and they experience reality very differently. They are far more different from us than people of different races, religions, political persuasions, and genders, and yet we can forge relationships with them, giving and receiving genuine Love. If we can befriend and Love animals, who are different from us in ways that are greater than we are different from each other, then surely we can learn to Love each other as well, despite our differences. This gives me hope.

Pupdate! Brandon has a home now! He's happy, healthy, and stable! It's several hours from Toronto so unfortunately, I don't get to visit him anymore, which is a little sad. But his family sends pictures and videos, so I know how he's doing. I think I'm going to send him a chew toy that I left in the laundry hamper overnight, so he has something to remember my scent by. I miss him, but I am *so* happy and relieved for him. He is very deserving of a Loving home, and he's got one now!

Foundations: Math, Science, and the Seven Virtues

Everyone then who hears these words of mine and does them will be like a wise man who built his house on the rock. And the rain fell, and the floods came, and the winds blew and beat on that house, but it did not fall, because it had been founded on the rock. And everyone who hears these words of mine and does not do them will be like a foolish man who built his house on the sand. And the rain fell, and the floods came, and the winds blew and beat against that house, and it fell, and great was the fall of it.

—Matthew 7:24-27 ESV.

The first modern dog training class I ever took was called Foundation Skills, and it was with a local training school that was run by a Karen Pryor Academy graduate named Andre Yeu. I was very happy with the class and was thinking about becoming a dog trainer myself. I had been grooming dogs and working in doggie day care for a few years already, but I knew little about dog training and behavior, which is really kind of horrifying. It seemed to me that understanding dog behavior and how dogs learn is something clearly foundational that should have been taught right at the beginning of any professional dog-care class or job.

When I had committed myself to becoming a dog trainer, the first class I had to take before I could even apply to their main dog trainer professional class was called Dog Trainer Foundations. It was a short online course that took about a month or so to complete and wasn't too expensive. It's a great starting place for anyone who wants to do any work with dogs. It's also a required prerequisite for anyone who isn't already training dogs and wants to take the Dog Trainer Professional Class and become a Karen Pryor Academy Certified Training Partner (KPA-CTP).

Both courses rely heavily on science. You are not going to get any magical sounding speeches about "your energy." There may be some mention of your emotional state and the importance of remaining calm, but it's all grounded in actual research. These classes are nothing like the vague pronouncements about your energy field and "balance" that uneducated trainers, pretending to be wizards or Jedi, like to casually throw around on TV shows that have disclaimers literally begging you "*not* to try this at home!" The KPA courses will teach you about how dogs learn. You will come to understand classical conditioning, operant conditioning, and counterconditioning, when and how these processes overlap, and how you can apply them.

They will also teach you the importance of being methodical. This was the part that was truly life-changing for me. I am not a methodical person by nature. I have always been a hard worker, but I didn't pay much attention to details. I was always looking for shortcuts, and I was not usually very thorough. One of the things I was instructed to do in the courses was to train with my dog for multiple short sessions every single day, track progress by keeping notes, saving the data, and using math. After we taught a dog a new behavior, we would set aside 10 treats, cue the behavior 10 times, and multiply the number of treats we give the dog by 10. So, if we gave the dog nine of the 10 treats, we know the dog can figure that cue out correctly 90% of the time in those exact circumstances. With a success rate that high, we can safely conclude the dog's got it, and we can increase criteria, adding some distractions (like a new location!), cueing from a distance, or increasing the duration. We work on distractions, distance, duration (or the "three D's"), stimulus control (responding correctly to the cue given), and we work on precision, and latency, speed (PaLS) to help the dog become "fluent" in the behavior, so it is reliable in nearly every situation.[29] This does not happen instantly; it takes a little work and sometimes a *lot* of patience. But the great thing about it is that you start making progress fast, and if you are keeping track, every time you make progress, you earn another reward for yourself: the satisfaction of knowing you and your dog learned something together. As a team. It's so much more powerful and rewarding than dominating your dog, making them submissive, and asserting yourself as the "alpha."

I think using pain and/or fear to motivate your dog is a shortcut, and a dangerous one. You can sometimes suppress an undesirable behavior very quickly with pain and fear; that's why it's so popular. But the risk of unintended consequences, and the potential damage it can do to your relationship with your dog, does not make it worth it. There is no way of knowing if your dog truly understands your punishment. If you hurt your dog because he barked, he *is not* going to understand that you did it because you don't want the people in the next apartment to make a noise complaint. There is a real chance that your dog will think sounds like doorbells and knocks make you angry with them, and your dog will hate those sounds *more*, not less. Most scientists now think spanking probably does more harm than good, but at least you can tell a person why you are punishing them; you can't do that with a dog. We do not share a common language, and the risk of misunderstanding and a damaged relationship is great. The scientific consensus on this fact is as overwhelming and clear as the scientific consensus on global warming. Don't rely on shortcuts. Trust the science, do the math, and do the work methodically. This is what I learned in a class called "Foundations."

At the time, I mentioned to my husband that I wanted to make myself a more methodical person. One of my fellow students showed up to our first workshop with a massive three ring binder with many color-coded sections separating all the material in the class into subject groups and leaving space to take notes and track progress. I was awestruck, and jealous! I never got as organized as she did, but I did start taking notes, and using math to track the results we were getting in our training sessions. The small amount of time it takes to do that is so worth it.

The name of that course, "Foundations," made a big impression on me. The importance of laying a solid foundation was drilled into me in ways I did not fully appreciate at the time, but it was around that time that I started to become a different person. "Foundations" became especially important to me. It was the organizing principle that guided major changes in my life. I took some yoga classes, worked with a personal trainer, made appointments with nutritionists, and started eating healthier. I started studying grammar and doing sentence diagrams. I had a lot to learn about grammar and still have a long way to go. I have so much more to learn about grammar that I was hesitant to mention that I've been studying it, because my grammar is still not great, and I imagined an editor looking at this book and saying, "You studied grammar and produced...*this!?!?*" There were so many errors in the first draft it was probably exhausting for my husband (who has great editorial skills!) to proofread it. Even though I still make a lot of mistakes, I am confident my understanding of grammar is better than it used to be, and better than most people's. Learning the basics about grammar, math, science, nutrition, and physical fitness made me a more confident person eventually, but it was not immediate. When you first start to learn new things, the realization of how much you don't know can be very intimidating. Thankfully, the earliest steps in any process of change are usually small, manageable steps. If you can learn the patience to avoid the temptation to cut corners and keep building on every small successful step, you can transform your life. Fitness instructors know this better than anyone. They are constantly telling people to pay more attention to form than weight. You need to make sure you are doing each exercise correctly, and not worry about how much weight you're lifting at first. That can be hard to do if you walk up to a machine and need to lower the weight by over 50% from what the last user was lifting. That always made me feel like a weakling, but I still tried my best to do things the right way. I have never had a bodybuilder's physique, but I am pretty fit these days, and I'm usually lifting just as much as the last person that used a machine at the gym before me, if not more. There are a few serious athletes at the gym who are half my age, and I will probably never be as fit as they are, but I am fit. I lost over 40 pounds in one year and am now physically stronger and in better condition than I have ever been in my life. The nutritionists and trainers that I spoke to were able to help me do this because they learned about the science of nutrition and exercise. They laid a solid foundation for me after making a career of pursuing those foundations themselves.

We need to reject the idea that math and science are stale, boring subjects, and instead celebrate them as foundational subjects that are beautiful and that we can all share. I mentioned in an earlier chapter how beautiful the formula 1=0.999... is to me. To many mathematicians, the left side of the equation points to the starting point for math, the number 1, whereas the right side represents the mystery of infinity, and the two sides are equal. Oneness=infinity. It sounds Buddhist to me, and I Love it.

Mathematician Edward Frenkel, in his book *Love and Math*, writes about the miracle of math:

> The fact that such objective and enduring knowledge exists (and moreover, belongs to all of us) is nothing short of a miracle. It suggests that mathematical concepts exist in a world separate from the physical and mental worlds—which is sometimes referred to as the Platonic world of mathematics. . . We still don't fully understand what it is and what drives mathematical discovery. But it's clear that this hidden reality is bound to play a larger and larger role in our lives, especially with the advent of computer technology and 3D printing.[30]

Some people have wondered if there could even be a formula that can mathematically express Love and have proposed several. Frenkel tells us, "Actually every formula we discover is a formula of love . . . And that's because these formulas represent something deep and fundamental about the world."[31] If you want to learn how to develop a real passion for math, you will want to read his book. His passion for math and the universal truths it reveals is intoxicating.

One of the best things we can learn from math is that reality is in fact logically ordered and does make sense. It may not appear to make sense to us a lot of the time because we don't know everything. But the mathematicians who become fluent in this universal language will see this truth more clearly than the rest of us do. As Charles Darwin famously noted in his autobiography, "I have deeply regretted that I did not proceed far enough at least to understand something of the great leading principles of mathematics, for men thus endowed seem to have an extra sense."[32]

If math and science represent a kind of universal language, what can we *do* with this language? What are the stories that we are going to uncover and tell? There is, of course, no guarantee we will tell *good* stories. This is why we need to study the virtues. Math can help to keep us honest; science can give us the power to do things that seemed impossible just a generation ago; but math and science are just tools, not virtues, and tools can be misused. Scientists can use their power for evil purposes, and there are many examples throughout history of scientists doing exactly that. Scientists are also subject to the same problems with confirmation bias that everyone else is, and they make mistakes all the time, just like everyone else. But scientists are skilled and experienced in the application of science, and we will never understand our world until we learn to trust them more and appreciate the foundation they have laid.

　　　　This foundational understanding of our world and reality is still incomplete. It will inevitably change over time as we learn more, and it can't really give our lives meaning. Only Love, virtuous living, and the Golden Rule can give our lives meaning. What is that meaning? What is... the meaning of Life?

Virtuous Mission

On January 1st, 2007, my beloved companion Kayla died in my arms after having a stroke. She was 19 years old and was the closest thing I've ever had to a child, and I Loved her dearly. Watching her die began one of the most painful years of my life. Shortly after, my mother and my sister Joyce were both diagnosed with cancer. My sister got better. I watched my mother die a little over a year after watching Kayla die. There have been eight times in my life I have been there in the room, watching while someone I Loved died. While part of me was glad to be there to say good-bye every time, it's a brutal, awful experience. When my mother died, I kind of snapped. I was angry, hateful even, and I was angry at, and felt a deeply intense hatred for, death. I swore under my breath, enraged, for about a minute. Then I hugged my dad and my brothers and sisters who were all there as well. I felt a dark cloud hanging over the room. It was like a thick, stifling presence, and I believed at the time that it was death, and that I could feel the presence of death itself in the room, and it had come to take my mother away from me. I have never been angrier. I have never hated anything more.

I hope I have made it clear that I think anger and hatred are dangerous things, and that if we allow these things to dominate our lives, they will destroy us. We should never hate any living thing, and we should be careful to save our anger for things like injustice, suffering, and our own worst behaviors, and not the character or personhood of others. But I will not stop hating death, and I will never accept it.

When Kayla died, I needed to find a job, and that's when I started working with dogs. I didn't want death to have the final word on my relationship with Kayla and dogs generally. I don't think it's true that "that which doesn't destroy you makes you stronger."[33] If you suffer a trauma, you are more likely to suffer PTSD than you are to be made stronger by it. But you can make yourself stronger by doing things, by setting goals and making progress, by solving problems and learning new things. Kayla's death weakened me. My response to her death, the goals I set and the work I put in, made me stronger. It was uneven: I had a lot of ups and downs, and I've since watched more people I Love die. But I am stronger now than I was when I was younger, and it's because I have laid a solid foundation: I have learned a new skill (dog training) and I am getting better at it. It all started with a class called "Foundation Skills."

I have even managed to save the lives of other dogs that were at risk due to behavioral problems. This will not bring back Kayla or my parents, but it will give me a reason to go on even in the face of the death of more people and animals that I Love, and my own eventual death.

I've spoken a lot about Christian religious traditions in this book, but right now I want to talk a little about Indian religious traditions. A philosophy teacher I had in college named Dr. Ed James explained to me that the religious philosophies of India start with the problem of pain, loss, and death. How do we deal with the fact that we all die, and eventually, as far as we can tell, we will be dead and gone for so long that no memory of us will exist anywhere in the universe? Everyone we ever Loved, everything we ever did: all lost, forever. Their approach

111

relies on non-attachment. Don't let yourselves become attached to the things of this life, so that when they are gone, you will not suffer from their loss. Christianity and other religions also caution us against being materialistic, but Hindu teachings in non-attachment go further than that. You can appreciate the things of this life while you are experiencing them, but don't hold on to them; accept that all of them, like you, will one day be gone, and allow for no attachment to them. This seems practical to me. Hindus believe in reincarnation and becoming one with Brahman (ultimate reality, god) as the two things that can happen to you after you die. Reincarnation is the less desirable outcome, because the cycle of life, death, rebirth, and the loss that it brings is a painful one. Becoming *one* with the ultimate reality is the goal. Becoming one with ultimate reality, or Brahman, does not mean you become a *part* of Brahman: it means *you become Brahman*. You are *not* a drop inserted into the ocean; you *are* the ocean. This view can offer some consolation in the face of death.

Ever since my college classes on Eastern philosophy I've always thought their understanding of the nature of the universal cycle of reality made sense. The scientific idea that the universe is in a constant cycle of expansion and contraction with an unknown number of Big Bangs setting off each new period of expansion sounds an awful lot like the Eastern philosophical tradition that we are all part of a universal cycle of death and rebirth.

Christians and most other adherents of Western religions have a belief in a Supreme Being who will raise us from the dead and restore us to a perfect state of being that will last forever. That is what I was raised to believe, and most of my life I did believe it. I couldn't logically justify those beliefs, but I felt quite certain. I felt certain because people I Loved and trusted told me so, but also because of three intensely powerful experiences I've had over the course of my life, in 1990, 2004, and 2009. They

112

are very difficult to describe, but they convinced me beyond any doubt that there was in fact an all-powerful creator God who Loved me and would set all things right. It was a beautiful, warm, comforting feeling. I am fairly certain a few skeptical readers will now say, "Oh, so he's a crazy person." Bear with me. I think I can change your mind about that.

Richard Dawkins, in his book *The God Delusion*, postulated that maybe people who experience spiritual conversion experiences are actually experiencing some rare condition, possibly related to epilepsy.[34] I was immediately uncomfortable with that explanation, but I also immediately recognized that it made sense. Just because I didn't know what happened to me was no reason to believe it was God. That's an important point that conspiracy theorists really struggle with: The fact that something is unknown is no reason to think your best guess is the actual truth; just the opposite, in fact. Your best guess is likely to be what you want to be true, rather than what *is* true. But that's not a trivial point. What we want to be true matters. Why did I want my experiences to be proof of God's existence? Why can't I just be honest enough to admit I don't know? The answer is because something inside me wants and even *needs* it to be true. It looks to me like the vast majority of people in this world have always wanted it to be true. No one wants to see someone they Love die and go away forever, eventually to be completely forgotten. No one wants to abandon their attachments to people and animals that they truly, deeply Love. We all want justice to reign; we all dream of and want a better world. No one wants to die, not even suicidal people; they just want not to live a little more. We all wish those we have Loved and lost to death will be reunited with us someday, and that we will all feel safe, and Loved, forever.

Immanuel Kant argued in favor of the immortality of the soul, as I discussed in the chapter "Virtuous

Animals?", by trying to prove that we *ought* to achieve moral perfection, because it is everyone's moral duty, and *ought* implies can. Since moral perfection is not achievable within a human lifetime, it is reasonable to believe in an afterlife.[35] Kant's notion of the highest good, what he called the "summum bonum," was a world in which everyone acted in accordance with the moral law, and everyone was happy, because they deserved to be. Kant also argued that since we can't create a world like that, then it's reasonable to believe that the source and foundation of this world will make it possible. He takes this to mean God. Kant did not think you could prove the existence of God and he disproved the most famous proofs for God that were used at the time.[36] Some people have guessed that Kant didn't really believe in God or the immortality of the soul, because he was so effective at disproving the arguments attempting to prove God and was a rigorous philosopher. But I think it's clear Kant believed morality was real and could be proven, and that it is our duty to strive for moral perfection. We may not be able to prove God exists, or that the soul is immortal, but if Kant is right that our highest good is to strive towards a world in which everyone is acting in accordance with the moral law and everyone is happy because they deserve to be, then it should at least be possible. I don't think we need to believe it is an intelligent creator God that makes this possible, although I do not think that belief is unreasonable. I don't know if it's true and being able to comfortably admit I don't know makes it easier to consider a range of possibilities. There is a freedom in knowing you don't know that I wish we all appreciated more often.

While I don't know if there is an afterlife, I do believe it, for the same reason Kant did. Looking across time and across different cultures, and their understanding of virtue and morality, I think it's clear we have moral obligations, and that we ought to strive for moral perfection. I don't know why we have this sense of duty: whether it's imposed by a God, or is simply a fact of our world like gravity, or if it's something else altogether. But I do believe we have a duty to strive towards moral perfection, and that if everyone becomes morally perfect and acts in accordance with the moral law, we will all be happy, because we will all deserve to be. I think we must strive for this state whether there is a God or not, and if it's ever achieved, then we will eventually be able to do literally anything, including create a world in which we are reunited with our Loved ones, and every tear is wiped away.

We do not, however, have the ability to make that happen ourselves, at least not yet. Sometimes you'll hear futurists talk about the technological singularity and how much they expect progress to speed up. Some even think they have a real shot at living long enough to be around when we are able to end death, and plan to bring back their parents using their DNA and all the memories they can store.

Ray Kurzweil is one of the most famous futurists, and seems like a brilliant man to me, a visionary even. He's one of the many brilliant, decent people trying their very best to make the world a better place. But this idea of raising the dead with computers seems a little silly to me. While I imagine it is possible that we *may* be able to clone people and upload memories into their brains some day in the future, this seems a little grotesque. The biggest problem is that this new cloned copy will not be the person you lost, even if it is a perfect replica. If you drop a lightbulb, and then make an absolutely perfect replica of that light bulb, the first light bulb is still going to be lying on the ground, broken into many pieces. Likewise, if you make a perfect copy of yourself and have it brought to life after you die, the original you is still going to be dead and buried, decomposing six feet under the ground, just like everyone else we've ever Loved so much that we desperately want to find a way to bring them back. *I don't want a carbon copy of my mom.* If someone were to make one, I have no idea how I would feel about that, but I would probably not be very happy that a copy was walking around calling itself Jean Josselyn while the real one was still dead. If it was really just like my mom, I would probably learn to Love her, but I would never stop wishing my real mother wasn't dead. *NEVER.*

But there's nothing I can do about that. She is dead, and I cannot bring her back. I also can't accept that, and I will not. I relive the deaths of every person I ever watched die every day, and I will never accept any of it. Maybe there is a God and a heaven, maybe we are all continuously reincarnated until we become one with Divine Reality, maybe futurists will be able to resurrect everyone with a supercomputer 50 years from now, and maybe *none* of that is true; maybe all the world's religions and transhumanists like Kurzweil are just wrong. None of us knows.

But one thing I think Kurzweil might be getting right is his answer to the question, "Does God exist?" His answer is, "Not yet."[37] I think his time frame is probably way off; he seems to think the technological singularity is imminent and the path to immortality is right around the corner. We are not anywhere close to being able to create something like the Heaven our spiritual traditions tell us waits for us after we die. But if we don't wipe ourselves out, who knows what will be possible a million years from now?

Kurzweil's dream of a computer heaven seems a little crazy to me and to a lot of other people too, and some of it *is* a little crazy; but if the pace of technological progress continues to accelerate, and the global trends showing wartime deaths, extreme poverty, and life expectancy continue to improve as they almost always do (Steven Pinker can prove this mathematically if you don't

116

believe it),[38] then what we think of now as being impossible *will* be possible someday: a heavenly realm where every tear is wiped away, where justice reigns, the dead are raised to eternal life, and death has been so far removed from the universe that no memory of the pain of death exists, and *no one* gets left behind, and *nothing* is lost. A place where, in the words of C. S. Lewis, we are forever going "farther up and farther in."[39] A similar phrase was used by Stan Lee to explain his use of the word "Excelsior!" at the end of every letter and tweet: "Upward and onward to greater glory!" is how he defined the word Excelsior.[40] I have Loved the stories told by C. S. Lewis and Stan Lee my entire life, and this is why: they both encouraged all of us to keep going onward and upward, to greater glory. The magical realms of Narnia and the Marvel Universe are only a reflection, like Plato's allegory of the cave, of the perfect world where everyone is *forever* moving onward and upward to greater glory. Or as Kant might say "endless progress" towards "complete conformity of the will with the moral law," where everyone is completely happy because they deserve to be.[41]

The pandemic and the recent rise in authoritarianism around the world can make it seem like we are currently going backwards, and not making progress at all. But we have survived pandemics and spreading authoritarianism before. We are likely to survive them again. Progress may be delayed, but it has not been halted. This past year has been a hard time, but it's not the end of anything.

Maybe God is not our Father, maybe he is our Children, maybe he is something we haven't even considered or couldn't possibly understand. I don't know. What I do feel certain about is something I was always taught as a child: "God is Love." The reason I always capitalize the word Love is because God is Love and Love is God, and we always capitalize "God" whether we're believers or not, because real and fictional names are capitalized. If there is no creator God, and no created God, then there will still be Love, and Love is the thing we need to make the heaven our ancient religions promised us a reality. I still attend an Anglican church, and a part of me still believes its traditional teachings. There is a symbolism and a beauty in the liturgy that is metaphorically true and that I will always Love. I still believe the person of Jesus Christ is one of the most important and inspiring in history. The Sermon on the Mount is one of the most important things ever written, so powerful and true that even Richard Dawkins himself once wrote an article called "Atheists for Jesus," and was later presented with a T-shirt bearing the legend.[42] I seriously doubt I could have written this book without the Sermon on the Mount and the Sermon on the Plain. Those two pieces are this book's foundation. But I can no longer say I believe in the existence of a creator God the way I once did. I'm not ruling it out, and I sometimes do still believe it to be true, but I can't say I believe it to be true the way I used to. I've learned to be comfortable saying, "I don't know."

If we were created by a God then our traditions teach us that this God wants *us* to make a perfect world with him, forever "farther up and farther in," like the end of the Narnia books by C. S. Lewis. In Narnia, the characters are asked to actively participate with Aslan/God in the continuing act of creation. The Narnia books end with everyone dying, but they don't realize it at first. They find themselves back in Narnia, but a better, more perfect Narnia where we're always getting better, still moving onward to greater glory with Aslan/God. *That's what I think the meaning of life, and any potential afterlife that may exist, is: moving continuously "onward and upward, to greater glory, farther up and farther in," forever.* This greater glory that we are moving towards, onward and upward, is more than just technological achievements, and it's not just competition or breaking records. It may include those things, but most importantly, it will be "endless progress" towards "complete conformity of the will with the moral law," where everyone is completely happy because they deserve to be.

If we were not created by God, and nothing like Heaven, Narnia, or Brahman exists, then we must make it so. Every culture on earth has been desperate for this since the dawn of civilization. No one really wants death to be the end of us all, forever.

There are some who claim they can be content with just this life. Richard Dawkins gives several examples of the consolation that the skeptical world view he supports can offer, and they are plainly *not good enough*.[43] Dawkins is clearly highly intelligent, but the consolation he offers is no consolation at all when you are watching someone you Love more than you Love yourself die before your eyes. There have been eight times in my life when I was in the room watching while someone I Loved died. Dawkins succeeded in opening the door to doubt for many people, but he failed at offering consolation to those frightened by what they saw when they opened that door. This chapter is meant to provide that consolation to all of us, whether we are believers or not.

If we live our lives virtuously, and work hard at it, we will find we can save lives, at least temporarily. We can extend the length of our days; we can make the world more just. We can make the world a little bit more like the vision of heaven our species has always dreamed of, using *math, science, and the seven virtues*. We are not going to create a world like heaven in our lifetimes; it's hard to even conceive creating a world like that from our flawed, limited perspective. But if we survive, if we don't wipe ourselves out, someday our descendants, *our children*, will be able to do *anything*, including put an end to suffering and death, raise the spirits of those that have died, and reach new, greater heights, forever and ever, onward and upward. If you have kids and grandkids, look into their eyes and Love them, because you just might be looking into the face of God.

If there is a creator God, and Christianity, or one of the other world religions, is true, then making this world more like heaven is exactly what we're supposed to be doing. I was taught this by my parents as a child. I read Immanuel Kant making the same argument when I was a college student. I re-learned these lessons after becoming a dog trainer. We were *not* taught to just open our hands and say, "Give me paradise, and make it snappy!" We were taught to work for it, to be co-creators with God in our world. One of my mom's favorite hymns was based on a prayer attributed to St. Francis, and it makes this exact point:

> Lord, make me an instrument of your peace:
> where there is hatred let me sow love;
> where there is injury, pardon;
> where there is doubt, faith;
> where there is despair, hope;
> where there is darkness, light;
> where there is sadness joy.
> O Divine Master, grant that I may not so much seek
> to be consoled as to console,
> to be understood, as to understand,
> to be loved. as to love.
> For it is in giving that we receive,
> It is in pardoning that we are pardoned,
> and it is in dying that we are born to eternal life.
> Amen.

That is one of the most beautiful, powerful, and inspirational things I've ever read. It also puts me in the mood for a fight, but not with people. Hatred, injustice, despair, division, and death are the things we are to live in opposition to. We must destroy those things, and not each other. I noted in the foreword that even after most of this book was completed, I had a few bad experiences and was struggling with depression. I am not struggling with it now, I am OK, *as I said I was* in the introduction. I also finished this book well before the end of summer, *as I said I would*, but nothing is over. I have no idea what the future holds. I will most likely experience tragedy, and doubt, many more times before I die. This past week, in the middle of the night, my car was set on fire by a random arsonist. The world is an unpredictable and scary place! I may lose to despair someday. But I do know that there are things I can do to make myself a more virtuous person, to resist my own worst impulses, and hopefully I can help others do the same. I can't guarantee any specific good outcome, but I know how to improve my chances. I know that nothing is guaranteed, but if I continue believing in the foundations written out in this book, and act on them, I will make it more likely that I can continue to grow as a person and become a *better, more perfect version of myself.*

That's what we all must do: patiently and methodically, never cutting corners, and laying a solid foundation using math, science, and virtue we must create *a better, more perfect world.* We must continue moving closer and closer to a more perfect world, one step at a time, methodically, with Love and joy in our hearts, even when it seems like the rest of the world is going backwards. If we do that, eventually, we will remake this existence into something like the heaven our ancestors promised us. We must work towards building a new reality that destroys suffering and death as completely and universally as we fear death is going to destroy all of us, until eventually, no memory of suffering and death exists anywhere. If there is a God, that God wants us to be co-creators in this perfect heaven with her. If there is no God, we must still work to create this perfect heavenly world, until our descendants become God. We need to hope for a better world and be willing to work to make it real.

That may seem impossible to some people, but we don't know enough to know what is and is not ultimately possible. If we survive long enough, eventually we will find ways to make impossible things possible, until nothing is impossible. As a popular ad campaign by Adidas featuring one of my great heroes, Muhammad Ali, puts it, "Impossible is just a big word thrown around by small men who find it easier to live in the world they've been given than to explore the power they have to change it. Impossible is not a fact. It's an opinion. Impossible is not a declaration. It's a dare. Impossible is potential. Impossible is temporary. Impossible is nothing."[44]

Dog bless you all.

Excelsior!

"This book is about how the Love I shared with . . . three dogs taught me how to cope with the pain of death and Love life again. My hope for this book is that it will help some people learn to Love their lives a little more too."

"So you may be wondering, is this book about dog training, science, Christianity, philosophy, or religion? It's about all those things, and how those things intersect in surprising and hopeful ways. This book is about living a good, virtuous, fulfilling life, and making the world a better, happier place for everyone. We can learn how to do that by looking at science, our history, our culture, and most importantly, at our own lives."

Dog trainer Dan Josselyn-Creighton reflects on his years of training, working with, and Loving dogs, and what these experiences have taught him about living a virtuous and happy life.

Taco 'bout the Author!

DANIEL JOSSELYN
KPA-CTP

  Dan Josselyn-Creighton is also the author of "Taco 'bout Training Tuesdays!" and has always had a passion for dogs, tacos, and talking about himself in the third person. Dan became a Karen Pryor Academy Certified Training Partner (KPA-CTP) in 2014 after spending several years as a dog groomer and doggie daycare attendant. Most dogs don't love being groomed, and many fear it, which is why he wanted to learn more about training and behavior so he could help make life easier for the dogs he worked with. Dan was also eager to help other groomers and dog owners teach their dogs to like being groomed instead of fearing it, so he also became Low Stress Certified through Dr. Sophia Yin's Cattle Dog Press, and more recently has been certified as a Fear Free trainer, groomer, and speaker. Dan's biggest heroes in the world of dog training are the doctors and scientists who have helped popularize modern, science-based dog training methods, like Dr Sophia Yin, Ian Dunbar, Patricia McConnell, Karen Overall, Marty Becker, and trainers specializing in behavior modification like Michael Shikashio and Grisha Stewart. His biggest hero, after his parents, is probably Mr. Rogers, because he thinks every person and every dog is special, just the way they are.

  Dan also appreciates the benefits of teaching dogs

fun tricks and games as a way of building up a dog's self-confidence, bonding with them, and improving their emotional well-being. Dan has taken classes on dog sports with Fenzi Dog Sports Academy and tricks with Kyra Sundance.

He first started eating tacos in his birth state of Massachusetts as a child and developed a love for tacos after his older sister Ellen started working in a Mexican restaurant. The first two things Dan learned to cook as a teenager were tacos and Kraft Dinner, or "mac and cheese" as we called it in Massachusetts. Dan eventually learned to cook more things after discovering that tacos, Kraft Dinner, and delivery pizza aren't actually the healthiest things in the world to eat, but still eats tacos every week on Taco Tuesday, and on Wednesday. Dan firmly believes that while tacos should be eaten every Taco Tuesday, it's OK to eat tacos on other days too. Any day that begins with a "T" is appropriate for tacos; this includes Tuesday, Thursday, Today, and Tomorrow.

Today Dan is the owner of Golden Rule Dog Training and teaches puppy socialization at Zendog on Church Street, virtual group classes and webinars with EduCanine, and especially loves giving private lessons to dog lovers in and around his neighborhood, Toronto's Church-Wellesley Village. He also volunteers some of his time with two dog rescue organizations, Coveted Canines Rescue (CCR) and Boston Terrier Rescue Canada (BTRC). CCR and BTRC are both volunteer-run nonprofits that save lives by helping dogs that need homes and homes that need dogs become families. Please take some time to see if there's any way you can support either or both of these wonderful organizations.

Acknowledgements

I would like to thank my spouse Jeff Josselyn-Creighton for all the work he did helping me on this book; I could not have written it without him. I also want to thank my friends Gwenda Jensen and John Stuart for their support, help, and encouragement. Most of all I want to thank my parents, Jean and Joe Josselyn, and my dogs, Kayla, Buffy, and Spike. Without them, I not only don't think I would have written this book, I also don't know if I'd even be here today. Thank you all and Dog Bless.

Endnotes

[1] S. J. Gould, "Nonoverlapping Magisteria," *Natural History* 106 (March 1997): 16-22 and 60-62.

[2] Sophia Yin, *What Giraffes, Dogs, and Chickens Have in Common,* Part 3, 3:53 (video lecture).

[3] Immanuel Kant, *Groundwork of the Metaphysics of Morals*, trans. and ed. by Mary Gregor (Cambridge: CUP, 1998), 4:429.

[4] Oxford Reference, "Utilitarianism," https://www.oxfordreference.com/view/10.1093/oi/authorit y.20110803114953685

[5] Jeremy Bentham, *An Introduction to the Principles of Morals and Legislation*, ed. J. H. Burns and H. L. A. Hart (Oxford: OUP, 1970), 283n.

[6] The Animal Behavior Network, "Canine Jolly Routine," http://www.animalbehavior.net/LIBRARY/Canine/PPM/D ogJollyRoutine.htm

[7] Barbara L. Fredrickson, "Why Choose Hope?" *Psychology Today,* 23 March 2009, https://www.psychologytoday.com/ca/blog/positivity/2009 03/why-choose-hope

[8] C. S. Lewis, *The Four Loves* (London: Geoffrey Bles, 1960), ch. 6.

[9] Aidan Bindoff, "Mission Impossible? How to Train 'Never Ever' Behaviors," Karen Pryor Clicker Training, 2013, https://www.clickertraining.com/node/1108

[10] Karen Pryor, "Shaping Your Way to Success," Karen Pryor Clicker Training, 2006, https://clickertraining.com/node/89

[11] Kayla Fratt, "Why We Punish Our Dogs," Journey Dog Training, https://journeydogtraining.com/why-we-punish-our-dogs/

[12] L. David Mech, "Alpha Status, Dominance, and Division of Labor in Wolf Packs," *Canadian Journal of Zoology* 77 (1999): 1196–1203, https://digitalcommons.unl.edu/usgsnpwrc/353
[13]

https://www.americanrhetoric.com/MovieSpeeches/moviespeechfridaynightlights2.html
[14] https://www.dictionary.com/browse/prudence
[15] Mick Foley, *Foley Is Good* (New York: ReganBooks, 2001), xii.
[16] Hara Estroff Marano, "Polite Company: A Chat with Judith Martin about Etiquette," *Psychology Today*, 1998, https://www.psychologytoday.com/ca/articles/199803/polite-company
[17] Mark Bekoff, "When Dogs Play, They Follow the Golden Rules of Fairness," *Psychology Today,* 2019, https://www.psychologytoday.com/us/blog/animal-emotions/201911/when-dogs-play-they-follow-the-golden-rules-fairness
[18] René Descartes, *Discourse on Method* (1637), Part V.
[19] European Commission, "Animal Welfare," https://ec.europa.eu/food/animals/animal-welfare_en
[20] David Kravetz, "No Habeas Corpus: Chimps Are Lab 'Property,'" *Ars Technica,.* https://arstechnica.com/tech-policy/2015/08/chimps-dont-have-same-legal-rights-as-humans-must-remain-in-research-lab/
[21] Helene Guldberg, "Animals Don't Have Morality, People Do," 2011, http://heleneguldberg.co.uk/animals-dont-have-morality-people-do
[22] Immanuel Kant, *Critique of Pure Reason*, 1787, A548/B576.
[23] "Postulates of Practical Reason" in "Immanuel Kant," *Internet Encyclopedia of Philosophy,* https://iep.utm.edu/kantview/#SH5c.; Immanuel Kant, *Critique of Practical Reason*, 1788, Part I Book II ch. IV.

[24] Roy F. Baumeister, "Free Will in Scientific Psychology," *Perspectives on Psychological Science* 3, no. 1 (2008): 14-19.

[25] Stephen Cave, "The Free-Will Scale," *Aeon,* 2015, https://aeon.co/essays/free-will-is-back-and-maybe-this-time-we-can-measure-it

[26] Stephen Cave, Free Will Exists and Is Measurable," *The Atlantic,* 2016, https://www.theatlantic.com/notes/2016/06/free-will-exists-and-is-measurable/486551/

[27] Charles Duhigg, *The Power of Habit* (Random House, 2014), 10ff.

[28] Mark Bekoff, "Will More Science Show It's Really OK to Harm Animals?" *Psychology Today,* 2018, https://www.psychologytoday.com/ca/blog/animal-emotions/201806/will-more-science-show-its-really-ok-harm-animals

[29] Casey Lomonaco, "Everything You Wanted to Know About Proofing—But Were Afraid to Ask," Karen Pryor Clicker Training, 2009, https://www.clickertraining.com/node/2279

[30] Edward Frenkel, *Love and Math* (New York: Basic Books, 2013), 23.

[31] "Searching for the Formula of Love," Big Think, 2014, https://bigthink.com/articles/searching-for-the-formula-of-love/

[32] Charles Darwin, *The Autobiography of Charles Darwin 1809–1882,* Ed. with appendix and notes by Nora Barlow (London: Collins. 1958), 58.

[33] Friedrich Nietzsche, *Twilight of the Idols* (1888), aphorism 8.

[34] Richard Dawkins, *The God Delusion* (London: Bantam, 2006), 168.

[35] See discussion in "Virtuous Animals?" and notes 22 and 23.

[36] "God (Ideal of Pure Reason)" in "Immanuel Kant," *Internet Encyclopedia of Philosophy,* https://iep.utm.edu/kantview/#SSH2giii

[37] John Rennie, "The Immortal Ambitions of Ray Kurzweil: A Review of Transcendent Man," *Scientific American* (2011), https://www.scientificamerican.com/article/the-immortal-ambitions-of-ray-kurzweil/

[38] 38. Steven Pinker, *Enlightenment Now* (New York: Penguin, 2018).

[39] C. S. Lewis, *The Last Battle* (Harmondsworth: Penguin, 1964), 146.

[40] Adam Epstein, "The Latin word Stan Lee made his life motto: "Excelsior!" *Quartz* (2018), https://qz.com/quartzy/1460772/the-meaning-of-excelsior-the-latin-word-marvel-legend-stan-lee-made-his-motto/

[41] Immanuel Kant, *Critique of Practical Reason* (1788), 5: 122.

[42] Dawkins, *The God Delusion,* 250.

[43] Dawkins, *The God Delusion,* 360-362.

[44] Aimee Lehto and Boyd Coyner, "Impossible Is Nothing," 2004. See: https://quoteinvestigator.com/2017/11/28/impossible-is/